COURSES FOR HORSES

COURSES FOR HORSES

A Complete Guide to Designing and Building Show Jumping Courses

Revised Edition

CHRISTOPHER COLDREY

J.A. ALLEN
London

Published in Great Britain by
J.A. Allen & Co. Ltd
1 Lower Grosvenor Place
London SW1W 0EL

First edition 1978
Revised edition 1991

British Library Cataloguing in Publication Data

Coldrey, Christopher
    Courses for horses: a complete guide to designing and
    building show jumping courses.—Rev. ed.
    1. Equestrian sports: Sports facilities
    I. Title
    798.25

ISBN 0-85131-541-0

Book design by Sandie Boccacci

Typeset in 10½/12 pt Palatino by
DP Photosetting, Aylesbury, Buckinghamshire
Printed and bound by
Biddles Ltd, Guildford

Contents

Acknowledgements

My grateful thanks are due to my son, Charles, who rode Alfoxton, and Anthony Reynolds LBIPP, LMPA, who took the action photographs for this book, including the lovely cover picture of John Whitaker and Milton at Hickstead. I am also grateful to John Birt, who took the pictures of the lovely fences at Badminton Horse Trials in 1991. Jon Doney was a great help with sound advice and discussion.

The diagrams from the first edition were drawn by John Monaghan and the photographs from that edition were by Peter Pilling.

Mo Kittermaster battled with the script, which she retyped in her usual flawless way. Richard Williams rode Persian Measure for some of the photographs.

Most of all it was my wife, Victoria, who helped get everything organised and put up with my constant disappearances to get it written, and to whom this book is gratefully dedicated.

Measurements

In Britain we are still, rather typically, in a bit of a muddle over metric and Imperial measurements. In this new edition metric measurements take pride of place, but in most cases Imperial equivalents are shown as well. The conversions are not exact, but are rounded off to make it easier and more logical to memorise. A few centimetres are not critical in the setting of distances between fences or when considering the length of a horse's stride, so the liberties taken in the cause of simplicity are of no practical significance. This particularly applies to the conversion of a single canter stride, which is traditionally 12 ft, using imperial measurements. The exact conversion is 3.65 m, but it is often shown as 3.50 m or 3.60 m.

With the above in mind, and as a quick reference, a conversion table based on a course designer's requirements is given in Appendix A at the end of this book.

Foreword to the First Edition

As Christopher Coldrey says, course building is an art as well as a science. It must be difficult enough to describe, in readable and clear form, the details and rules which make up the 'scientific' side, but far harder to convey the need for flair and imagination which distinguish the artist from the plain cook.

The author has succeeded admirably in both these tasks. He can call on the experience of course building for twenty-five years in seven different countries and two different continents, Europe and Southern Africa. He has thought deeply about the problems involved, and possesses an exceptional facility as a writer.

His book is clear, interesting, readable, and extremely informative. I commend it not only to course builders but to show executives, judges and officials, and to all those interested in and participating in the sport of show jumping.

General Sir Cecil Blacker, GCB, OBE, MC
1978

Foreword to the Second Edition

Chris Coldrey has gained the knowledge to write this book after many years working with horses as a rider, show organiser and international course designer. His feel and love for animals is such that he would never construct a course without realising the capabilities of the horses which are going to attempt it. I have always harboured a desire to write a comprehensive book on course designing and building, but every time I have started putting pen to paper, I have decided it is so complicated and would need so much explaining that I have given up the idea. Furthermore, when I read the first edition of this book, I realised that Chris's ideas were so much in line with my views, and so well explained, that I gave up the thought altogether.

Now with this up-dated and more informative second edition, including several new chapters, there is no need to clutter your bookshelves with any other volume on the subject. This book not only explains Chris's beliefs in detail, but also covers many other ideas by course designers of world standing.

Of course, not all designers will agree with every detail, but this book will be a good 'bible' for anyone competing in the Novice levels to the top international competitions, and covers both international show jumping and the show jumping section of eventing.

This book is not just for course builders; it is a very useful guide for competitors and trainers. Having an insight into what designers are trying to achieve can only help trainers and riders to overcome some of their riding problems. There have never been enough good educational books on this subject, but this is one which covers all aspects in the greatest detail.

John F. Doney
1991

Introduction

Designing and building show jumping courses is an addiction. Like any drug, once it has you hooked it will never let you go. Heaven only knows why. Course building is exhausting, nerve racking, often dirty and cold or dusty and hot. When everyone else has departed at the end of the day the course builder and his team are still beavering away for tomorrow while everyone else is relaxing over a drink, soaking in a warm bath, or debating the successes and failures of the day's sport. You need the energy of an athlete, the hide of a rhinoceros, the sensitivity of an antenna, the courage of your convictions and a limitless sense of humour. Notwithstanding all this, course building is endlessly fascinating and richly rewarding.

A course designer is like an architect. The architect must have the necessary training and technical knowledge before he can start his design. With this background he, or any architect, should be able to produce a building that adequately serves its purpose. In the same way anyone can learn to produce a jumpable course. But only an architect with exceptional talent could produce Coventry Cathedral, and in the same way it takes much more than technique to set great show jumping courses. Course designing is, then, an art as well as a science.

The purpose of this book is to provide some of the technical information on which course designing has to be based; to express some of the conclusions that I have drawn from building courses (and studying those of others) in twelve countries over nearly forty years and, most important of all, to give expression to some ideas that will help the individual flair and personality of each individual designer to flourish. It would be very boring if all course designers built alike. There are few rights and wrongs – just courses that produce marvellous jumping, good jumping or bad jumping.

The problem is that in most countries today there are far more jumping shows than good course builders. Naturally, the more important shows get the leading authorities to design their courses. This means that at smaller events inexperienced course designers are often engaged with the result that novice horses are put off just when they need most encouragement, by ill-conceived tracks over inadequate fences. Often novice course designers graduate from the ranks of enthusiastic pole-pickers-up and start their career without having been asked to think constructively about what their objectives are. In Chapter 1 these objectives are spelt out and from them a definition of a good course is derived.

In this book I have tried to follow a logical sequence. After outlining the principles and ideals that are the basis for setting successful courses, I have analysed the actual performance of the horse over different types of obstacle and so produced proven information from which the course designer can work out his own tracks and choose his own tests. The sequence then follows through with background information and systems that will help to produce courses that are attractive to ride and to watch.

In this new and enlarged edition there are four major additions. I have asked a number of the best designers in the world to send plans of one of their major courses with details and their thoughts at the time. They are of great interest and emphasise to perfection the artistic and individual approach that makes one course designer quite different from another. I have also included a chapter on courses for horse trials. For this Jon Doney has contributed details of his courses at Badminton in 1989 and 1990. I regard these as the ultimate in horse trials building and an example to us all. A new chapter has also been written about building for working hunters and working hunter ponies. It can be fun planning and building these, and a bit of imagination can produce an excellent crowd-pleaser as well as a good test of a hunter. The other addition is a description of a seminar that we ran at Herringswell Bloodstock Centre with Alan Ball. I have included the timetable and a description of everything that we did as it might be found useful by others running a similar teach-in. I believe that it was very effective as well as greatly enjoyed by everyone who took part.

If course designers need to understand the body and mind of the horse, so, even more, must the rider. I hope that this book will not only prove of interest and value to course designers but also to riders for, if they understand how courses are planned, they will be able to read a course in a more educated way and so ride it more effectively. It must clearly follow that trainers of show jumpers should understand all the principles and have a knowledge of all the technical data described in this book in order to set schooling fences and gymnastics, as well as to help their students to achieve a good result over courses. To this end I have included as Appendix D a set of diagrams of exercises for show jumpers over trotting poles, grids and gymnastics.

There are two different kinds of horse show. One is planned to attract and entertain spectators and the other is to provide a training facility. At the latter kind of show the course designer has only one responsibility and that is towards horse and rider. At the former kind of show it is quite a different matter. The course designer's main role is to provide spectacular entertainment in an arena that is as aesthetically satisfying as it can possibly be made with the material available to him. How these two problems should be tackled will be one of the main themes of this book.

Photo 1 *The author.*

1 ◇ *A Course Designer's Philosophy*

The first question that a course designer must ask himself is: 'What am I trying to achieve?'

It really is not a matter of arriving on the showground on the morning of the show with an empty mind, putting up a few jumps from a set of often inadequate material and hoping that good riders will save you from your own lack of enthusiasm.

Genius is the infinite capacity for taking pains. To produce good tracks for even the smallest show means a great deal of preparation: a visit to the ground before planning starts; a list of material available; thought on how to improve its presentation; thorough planning on paper, for every class and for every change of course during the day; a time schedule of events, together with the anticipated number of starters, so that you can plan to keep the show running to time; and much much more.

The course designer must set himself five objectives. An objective is a target or a goal and it is one where success can be measured. In other words at the end of the day the question: 'Did I or did I not achieve what I set out to do?', can be answered.

We must now look at these five objectives, and their definitions, in a little more detail.

OBJECTIVE 1   **'To produce an exciting event for spectators with a high standard of jumping and a thrilling finish.'**

A good course is one that is well ridden. *If it does not produce good jumping never blame the riders or horses, blame yourself.* A course that is good for one set of competitors can be a disaster for those of a different calibre. This applies not only to the size of the fences but also to the track taken by the horse. Simplicity is the essence of a good course and the more inexperienced the horse the more straightforward must be the track.

More will be said in Chapter 5 about the number of fences and the length of the course but, in order to produce a thrilling finish, the course must end on a high note. Never finish a course with two or three fences that are very unlikely to produce any faults. Your competition must work to a climax of excitement, which is why a class with one jump-off is the surest way of achieving success. In the same way, the course must work to a climax which produces a sigh of relief as the horse clears the last fence – or a groan of sympathy if it does not.

Combinations of fences, too, should work to a climax. The point of the test is the third element. Obviously, in a great competition all three elements will be testing, but in normal events the first fence invites the horse to jump in boldly, the second fence tests his control and courage and the third tests his scope. Once again, combinations should aim to produce a sigh of relief or a groan of dismay as the climax (the third element) is reached.

Thus, in achieving excitement and a thrilling finish, there are three climaxes the course designer can use – a climactic end to the competition, to each round over the course and to each combination or line of fences.

OBJECTIVE 2 **'To give riders a sense of achievement and satisfaction at the end of each round, even if they have had faults.'**

The essence of good horsemanship in all disciplines is rhythm. A show jumping course should therefore invite the competitor to produce a flowing and rhythmical round. The horse moves forward with controlled and steady power and is not pulled about and ridden with constant STOP-GO messages from the rider.

It is a true test of a great course if a competent rider can come out of the ring with a couple of fences down, slapping his horse on the neck and saying: 'Didn't he jump well?' Horses and riders love a challenge – provided it is a fair challenge. They get a far greater sense of achievement from jumping bigger fences (relative to their grade and experience) on a flowing track with fair approaches to fences than having to pull a horse's head about over smaller misplaced jumps.

OBJECTIVE 3 **'To cause as few eliminations as possible, but still achieve the number of clear rounds required by the type of event.'**

I hate to see disastrous falls in the arena and if they occur more than very rarely the course designer must search his conscience. They will happen, inevitably, but the idea that it is what spectators come for is wrong. They know the risk is there and what they want to see is danger overcome. As in most sports, what spectators are looking for is something that they would like to do but can't – so it is great artistry in the teeth of danger that provides the exhilaration. It is the setting for this that the show organiser and the course builder provide.

So, the first measure of achievement of this objective is to have few eliminations while maintaining the idea that the course is a test over which the competitor must triumph. Incidentally, the commentator can help here enormously because people almost invariably believe what they are told and can be made to feel the excitement of the challenge they see presented to horse and rider.

Different standards of competition demand different numbers of clear rounds.

At a riders' show with few spectators the only criterion is the time allocated for the class. For novices about one third of the starters should go clear in the first round. In spectator classes, with a first round followed by a jump-off, you must get enough clear rounds to produce an exciting end to the competition. I do not personally go along with the idea that a course has proved too easy if it produces between five and eight clear rounds. This gives you an almost certain guarantee of a really thrilling jump-off. With fewer you are at risk; with more you are likely to make it boring. Of course, the number of starters must be taken into account, but if you get five clear from a field of twenty-five and eight clear from a field of forty you won't be far wrong. How to set about this is dealt with in Chapter 5, but these figures give the course builder an objective to aim for in normal circumstances.

OBJECTIVE 4   'To help organisers by keeping to time.'

The course designer can achieve more towards this end in his homework and preparation than at the show itself. First the arena must be absolutely ready an hour before the first competition is due to begin. If possible I like to have my arena finished the day before, not only because it takes a weight off my mind, but also because I like the arena to look its best as competitors and officials arrive on the showground. The longer you have after your first course is up, the more preparation you can make for subsequent changes of course.

It is fundamental that you change the course for every class. It takes a good deal of careful thought and planning, but a good builder can have a quite major change completed before the prize-giving for the previous class is over. He must always think one stage ahead of what is happening. For example, during the first round of a competition the arena party can be briefed on what is to be done to reset for the jump-off. And during the jump-off itself, fences not in use can be prepared for the next class (but don't disturb a competitor in the ring, nor distract the eye of spectators), whilst during the prize-giving the fences that were used in the jump-off are made ready.

The course itself must be designed to fit the time allocated. If time is tight do not set too long a track with too many fences. Place the start so that the next horse to go can be ready as soon as the last has left the arena – but remember not to start by asking horses (especially novices) to set off away from the entrance (see Chapter 4). Similarly, the finish should not be so far from the exit that it takes a long time to trot out at the end of a round.

OBJECTIVE 5   'To criticise your own course after the event according to how it achieved these objectives.'

Ask yourself the following questions:

- 'Was each competition exciting?'
- 'Did they all finish with a climax?'
- 'Was the jumping excellent?'
- 'Did horses perform above or below their normal standard?'
- 'How many horses were eliminated and why?'
- 'Did the show run to time?'
- 'If not, was it my fault?'

These are just some of the questions that the conscientious course builder will ask himself after *every day of every show*. If the answers are not what you would like them to be you must discover the reason and note the lessons learned for the future.

Course building is like riding – you never stop learning, and if you think you know all about it then it is time to give up. A course builder must be his own most severe critic and there can be no excuses. Either the course met the objectives set or it didn't, and if it didn't, it wasn't right.

Course designers come in for criticism, often justified, sometimes not. Listen to criticism and accept it if you can after the event. Once you are sure that you are satisfied with your course before a class, do not let outside pressure make you change it (unless ordered to do so by the judge – on which more later). My experience is that changes – especially as the result of pressure from individual competitors – are nearly always a mistake and that it is best to stick to your guns. *But* if you don't make the change, and are then proved wrong, for heaven's sake admit it and learn from it. You are building courses for brave riders and horses of great value and there is no room for anyone who irresponsibly or ignorantly places either at risk.

From the five objectives we have discussed a definition of a good course can now be found. It is that: success is achieved when a course produces atmosphere and excitement among spectators, a sense of exaltation and achievement in the riders, and confidence and enthusiasm in the horse.

2 ◇ How a Horse Jumps

I think that many course builders tend to build 'parrot fashion'. There are plenty of pamphlets and articles produced which list standard, recommended distances between various types of fence. Inexperienced course builders, or perhaps those for whom the job has become too much a matter of routine, will take these distances for granted and set them up without ever actually analysing what they are doing and why. This probably works out pretty well over small tracks but to achieve greatness a real understanding of the factors that affect how a horse jumps is imperative.

The shape of a fence dictates absolutely the shape of the horse's flight. The angle of descent dictates the length of the stride after landing. The nature of a fence, or a series of fences, serves to increase or decrease the impulsion (forward momentum) of the horse at a given point. The mental limitations of the horse will tend to make him jump differently in different parts of the arena, depending upon what stage his training has reached.

In this chapter these are some of the factors that are studied and it is from this factual information that course designers can begin to derive the tests that they choose to set. Remember that the more adventurous you become, the more certain you must be of your facts. When setting unusual tests you may not be quite sure of the outcome, so don't make them too severe until you have watched them jumped and have carefully studied the results. At the end of this chapter is an analysis of two fences from the Hickstead Derby which illustrates the importance of this point (Fig. 9).

First let us look at the basics. There are three types of fence; upright, or vertical, fences; parallel fences; and staircase fences.

UPRIGHT, OR VERTICAL, FENCES

These fences will include upright rails, straight walls, planks and so on. They are the most difficult to jump, requiring the greatest accuracy from horse and rider.

At a vertical the horse takes off and lands the same distance from the fence, and the highest point of his flight is exactly over the top of the fence (see Fig. 1).

There are countless ways of presenting vertical fences. The stronger the groundline, the easier it becomes. If the fence is to be a true vertical, the groundline should never be pulled forward from the vertical plane. We can see this

Photos 2–5 *Vertical fence. The white lines are 1.8 m (6 ft) on either side on this vertical fence. Charles Coldrey and Alfoxton demonstrate the theory explained on pages 17 and 20.*

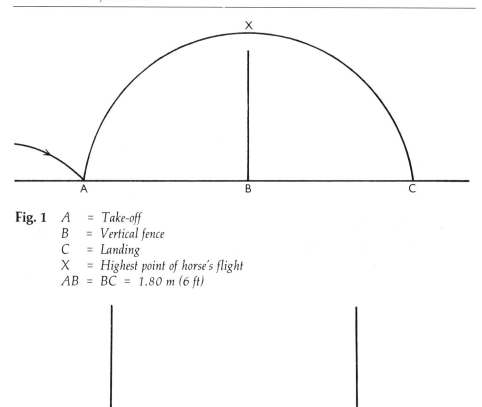

Fig. 1   *A* = *Take-off*
           B = *Vertical fence*
           C = *Landing*
           X = *Highest point of horse's flight*
          AB = *BC* = *1.80 m (6 ft)*

Fig. 2   *In case A the groundline is in front of the vertical, which makes a much easier fence than in case B where the front of the fence is absolutely straight.*

by studying Fig. 2. In case A the groundline is in front of the vertical which makes a much easier fence than in case B.

It is accepted that in the early stages of training a horse he must be taught to make his own stride arrangements in the approach to a fence. Just as a child kicking a football measures his strides in running up to the ball instinctively, so a horse's mind must automatically compute stride and distance to take off at the right point to clear the fence. In his very early training, by all means give the horse every opportunity to get his fences right, but once he is in the ring I believe that vertical fences should be absolutely straight.

An interesting point, and one that is not always appreciated, is that anything forward of the line of the fence, even at the wings, makes the fence easier to jump. Fig. 3 explains this point clearly, being a plan view of three different presentations of the same vertical fence. By changing the positions of the wings and the shrubs three quite different problems are set. The angled wing helps a horse to take off

Photos 6–7   Above: *A vertical fence made easier by enclosing the approach with wings.* Below: *The same fence made harder by straightening the wings.*

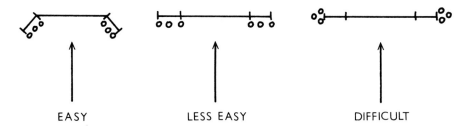

EASY   LESS EASY   DIFFICULT

Fig. 3 *Plan view of three different presentations of the same vertical fence. By changing the positions of the wings and shrubs three different problems are set.*

and, by giving him a sense of being enclosed, also makes him tuck up his hind legs over the fence.

Indeed, an exercise that is designed specifically to make a horse tuck up his hind legs is an exaggeration of the angled wing. Two poles are placed as a funnel on the take-off side of the fence and resting on the front rail (see Fig. 4). I have never known a horse knock this down and I must have used it a thousand times in training. So the more a fence is built like this, the easier it becomes. Thus prominent angled wings will always help a horse to jump.

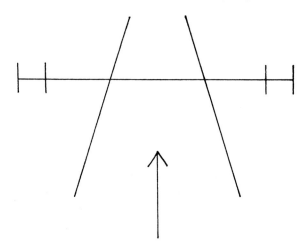

Fig. 4 *This exercise can be used over both vertical and parallel fences and is demonstrated in Photos 8 and 9.*

PARALLEL FENCES

A parallel fence is a spread fence whose front and back elements are the same height. A true parallel is more difficult than an ascending one where the front element is slightly lower than the back. The back pole should *never* be lower than the front.

Photo 8   *Alfoxton jumps the funnel of poles.*

Photo 9   *He has really flexed his hind fetlock joints and hocks. There is no danger of touching this fence.*

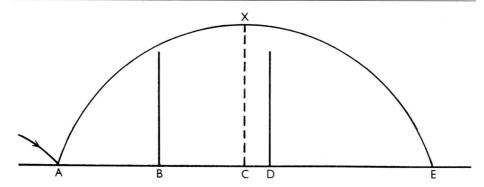

Fig. 5 A = *Take-off*
B = *Front element of a parallel fence*
CX = *Highest point of horse's flight*
D = *Back element of a parallel fence*
E = *Landing*
AB is shorter than DE
AC = CE ≏ 2.40 m (8 ft)

At a parallel the horse takes off nearer and lands further out from the fence than at a vertical. The top of his flight is closer to the back element than the front (see Fig. 5). Exactly the same points concerning the groundline and presentation of the fence apply to the front element of a parallel as to the vertical fence. If the parallel fence is made into an oxer by putting filling into the middle, there is a danger of giving a false groundline. (This should never be done in novice classes, when a strong groundline which hides the base of the filling should be used.) It is a legitimate test for advanced horses and will bring faults.

I never use more than a single pole at the back of a parallel. This is an important safety precaution and saves damage and injury if a horse should fail to make the spread. On no account should a plank be used in place of a pole.

Many riders fight shy of wide parallels and I have often seen pressure put on course builders by riders to pull them in. The result is that when riders are faced with big spreads at major shows they find them unnecessarily off-putting.

The fence over which a horse covers the least ground from take-off to landing is a narrow upright fence such as a stile. Over such a fence standing at, say, 1.15 m (3 ft 9 ins) the average distance jumped will be 4 m (13 ft). Over a parallel fence 1.20 m (4 ft) square the average jump will cover about 5 m (16 ft).

Figures 6 and 7 show how in these cases, given the same jump, it would have made no difference if the narrow fence had been a parallel 1.40 m (4 ft 6 ins) wide and the 1.20 m (4 ft) parallel had been 2.10 m (7 ft). Let us look at these in more detail.

In Fig. 6 B is a stile 1.15 m (3 ft 9 ins) high, A is the take-off point, and C is the landing. The dotted lines at D show that the same jump would have cleared a parallel of stiles with a 1.40 m (4 ft 6 ins) spread – and this is the type of fence over

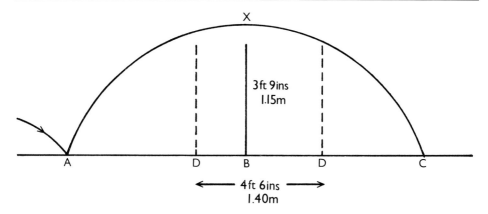

Fig. 6 *B is a stile 1.15 m (3 ft 9 ins) high. A = take-off; C = landing. The dotted lines at D show that the same jump would have cleared a parallel of stiles with a 1.40 m (4 ft 6 ins) spread – and this is the type of fence over which horses make the shortest jump of all.*

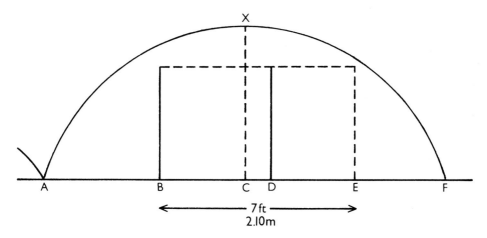

Fig. 7 *A horse covering 5 m (16 ft) when jumping a 1.20 m (4 ft) square parallel would, with the same jump, still jump clear if the parallel had been 2.10 m (7 ft) wide.*
AC = CF ≏ 2.40 m (8 ft)
BD = 1.20 m (4 ft)
BE = 2.10 m (7ft)

which horses make the shortest jump of all.

Figure 7 shows that a horse covering 5 m (16 ft) in jumping a 1.20 m (4 ft) square parallel would, with the same jump, still have been clear had the parallel been 2.10 m (7 ft) wide.

I am NOT suggesting that parallels should be pulled out to 2 m (6 ft 6 ins) or more. I am suggesting that course builders can look at the mathematics of this,

Photos 10–13   *Parallel fence. The white lines are now 1.20 m (4 ft) in front of the fence and 2.40 m (8 ft) beyond the fence. The top of the horse's flight is just in front of the back element of this parallel fence.*

understand the principle and so draw their own conclusions. Fairly low, wide parallels do get horses jumping correctly and really using their head, neck and back. I like to put a wide, low parallel at the end of a line of fences going towards the exit, even in novice classes. It is always jumped really well and fills both horse and rider with confidence.

Riders are encouraged by this sort of fence to give their horse freedom to stretch the head and neck. This freedom is very important. The horse's head is extremely heavy and in the parabola of the flight over a fence acts like a conker on the end of a string. If given freedom it serves to draw the horse's body in an arc over the fence, making a fault very unlikely.

I was once teaching a class of beginners over a small gymnastic exercise of four trotting poles followed by a low parallel .75 m (2 ft 6 ins) high and 1.20 m (4 ft) wide. A child on a small dun novice pony got a big jump which we measured at 5.70 m (19 ft) from take-off to landing. She was more than surprised to learn that she had just cleared the Olympic Games water jump by a metre out of a trot. Wide spreads need not be the bogey that they sometimes seem – especially if they have been sensibly used in training and in good courses at all stages.

STAIRCASE FENCES

A staircase fence is a spread that is lower in front than behind. The extreme example is the triple bar. They are the easiest type of fence to jump.

At a spread fence the lower the front element, the closer the take-off point. The high point of the horse's flight moves back and is over the highest part of the fence, and the landing is further out again from the fence (see Fig. 8).

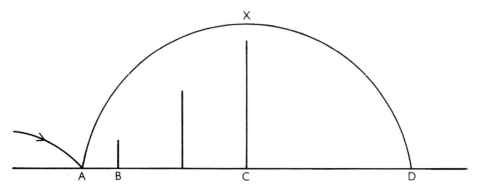

Fig. 8   *AB is much shorter than CD; AC = CD ≃ 2.75 m (9 ft).*

SUMMARY

Figures 1 to 8 show how the nature of the fence dictates the point at which a horse will take off. The take-off point will be further out from a vertical than a parallel, and further from a parallel than a staircase. The arc described by the horse's flight reaches its highest point directly over a vertical fence, just in front of the back pole of a parallel and directly over the back element of a triple bar. This arc is steeper over an upright and flatter over a triple bar. So a horse will land closer to the back of a vertical fence, a little further out from a parallel and further still from a triple bar. An understanding of this principle is necessary for the correct placing of fences in combination and at closely related distances.

The distance covered by the jump over any fence is approximately 3.50 m (12 ft) plus the width of the fence.

STRIDE AFTER LANDING

In Chapter 6 detailed consideration is given to the setting of tests with fences at related distances. At this stage, though, thought must be given to how the nature of a fence affects the length of the horse's stride after landing.

The steeper the landing, the shorter will be the next stride. There is little difference over small fences jumped off a normal stride, but as the fences get bigger the difference becomes more marked.

On landing steeply over a vertical of, say, 1.60 m (5 ft 3 ins) the next stride will probably average 3.30 m (11 ft) compared to the 3.60 m (12 ft) which is a normal canter stride. If the vertical was in combination with another fence a difference of this kind could have a huge effect.

Contrariwise, the shallow arc followed by a horse over a triple bar results not only in landing farther out from the fence but also in a longer subsequent stride.

There are several other factors affecting length of stride and impulsion which are also critical in selecting distances between fences in combination. These also are dealt with in Chapter 6.

At the beginning of this chapter I mentioned the importance of studying what actually happens when setting an unusual test and not making such tests difficult until you are sure of the outcome. A good example of such a test is that set in the Derby at Hickstead. One of the most exciting parts of the course is the drop down

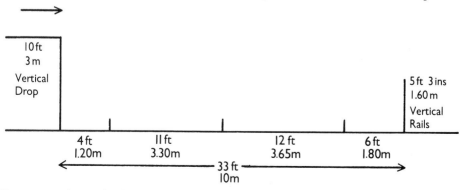

Fig. 9 *Derby Bank followed by vertical.*

Photos 14–17 *Triple bar. The white lines are now 60 cm (2 ft) in front of the fence and 3 m (10 ft) beyond the fence. The high point of the horse's flight is right over the back element of the fence.*

the Derby Bank followed the three flights of white rails. This is shown in Fig. 9 where an almost sheer drop of 3 m (10 ft) is followed after 10 m (33 ft) by 1.60 m (5 ft 3 ins) vertical rails. You can work out the striding in many different ways, the crux of the matter being how they come off the bank. It is virtually impossible to say exactly what will happen but experience of this particular problem shows that a distance of 10 m (33 ft) is right. It would be madness for an inexperienced course designer to set a problem of this severity on the basis only of calculations on paper.

In this chapter I have dealt with some of the fundamental technicalities of jumping. This is vital information which any course designer must have before he can start on his job.

So far then, we have set objectives, defined good courses and investigated how a horse jumps. Before we come to an examination of setting tests within the framework of a course, we must discuss the role of the course designer and arrive at some simple principles and guidelines which are generally accepted, if not always followed.

3 ◇ The Role of the Course Designer

The job of the course designer starts long before the show and he has a crucial function to perform in three phases of the planning. If he lives far away it may not be possible for him to be consulted, but his part in the planning must be carefully considered by the show committee. The three phases are:

- Choice of ground.
- Preparation of fences.
- Planning the programme.

This does not just apply to major shows but to every show that is to be successful, and a good and conscientious course designer will take as much trouble and pride in his work at a one-day local event as at an international.

Let us look at these three phases of planning in more detail.

CHOICE OF GROUND

Many shows are not held in the formal surroundings of a stadium, but rather on a piece of farm or park land generously made available to the committee for their one event a year. The area must be examined with the eye of an artist and laid out, not only from the viewpoint of functional efficiency, but also as the setting for a great occasion. The arena is the stage for an outdoor entertainment and a beautiful backcloth adds something very special.

Flatness is not necessarily the only criterion in choice of ground. For example, I love to incorporate a hedge, a depression or gully, or to find two levels with a sloping bank between. Jumping can be made more interesting for spectators, more attractive to watch, stimulating for horse and rider and the subject of interesting discussion and a source of new ideas.

Sensible and moderate use of ground can achieve a good result without having to test every horse to the limit of its scope. As a result of the very high standard of show jumping today, even at national level, course designers tend to build very big fences in order to avoid getting too many clear rounds. Use of ground is one way to alleviate this problem. Other ways are discussed in Chapter 5.

In Germany, show jumping is called '*Jagdspringen*', which means 'hunt jumping'. The origins of show jumping, everywhere in the world, lie in the hunting field and modern fences are notional representations of natural cross-country obstacles.

Many Continental arenas have for years included slopes, ramps and banks to a far greater extent than those in Britain. Indeed, they were virtually unknown in Britain until introduced at Hickstead, in 1959, with the opening of the glorious All-England Jumping Ground.

Slopes, if used with discretion, serve to make jumping more exciting for the public, provide a refreshing change for the horses, offer a new challenge for the riders, and are a great help to the course designer. Arena North featured such slopes. Jan Brouwer, Dutch judge at the Bass Young Riders International Horse Show there in 1974, wrote of 'this beautiful and unique arena, which enables any course builder to develop other and more attractive courses than he probably has ever done before!'

Going downhill a horse's balance is likely to drop on to his forehand and he is liable to hit a fence at the bottom of the slope in front. Conversely, going uphill he will tend to get strung out and dismantle a fence, especially a wide oxer, at the top of the slope through failing to get his hind legs quickly up underneath him. Clearly the length of stride is shorter going uphill and longer going down. Course designers should study this effect and be able to gauge it accurately before placing fences close together on sloping ground.

Variety is the spice of life and a designer must be prepared to build in whatever profile the arena has. Sometimes he is lucky enough to be able to help a committee to choose the ground, and he must look at it with the eye of an artist while bearing in mind the technical problems that will confront him.

If some arenas incorporate sloping ground, some have permanent obstacles, such as Hickstead and Hamburg, and some are traditional on flat, level turf, the range of skills demanded of competitors will be widened to the benefit of the sport.

It is likely that any organisation planning to set up a show jumping arena will call on course builders for advice. Some points to help are:

Minimum size outdoors = 90 m (100 yds) × 75 m (80 yds). If the arena is small, less than 135 m (150 yds) × 110 m (120 yds), do not use too many permanent fences except a water jump. This inhibits the freedom of the course builder to use the ground as he may wish.

If the arena includes sloping ground it should also have the minimum area for an outdoor arena, 90 m (100 yds) × 75 m (80 yds), on one, flat level for conventional use, dressage exhibitions and displays.

PREPARATION OF FENCES

The responsibility of the committee organising a show is clear. They must discuss with the course designer his requirements as to materials, well before the show itself. What is more they must produce them ready for him to put up at the appropriate time. This is not so difficult at a permanent showground, but is a mammoth task at a weekend event, for example, where the jumping equipment is borrowed or hired. The most talented builder cannot make a silk purse out of a sow's ear and if organisers want a super show they must set to and produce the necessary material. A list of equipment needed for a major show is given at the end of this chapter (see Table 1).

In many countries the national bodies responsible for show jumping have sets of fences available for hire and during the season these often-used fences deteriorate rapidly, for nothing is so destructive as loading and off loading. The availability of sets of fences for hire is a mixed blessing because show committees tend to think that if they hire such a set they have done their job. They have only done half of it. In addition to the actual show jumps themselves, shrubs, pot plants and decorative fillers still have to be obtained. And when material arrives it must be assembled (this is very definitely the job of the committee and not the course designer), and when it has been assembled it will almost certainly need the attention of a painter for at least a day to touch up and improve the appearance of the fences, which must also have time to dry before the arena party sets to work.

In Chapter 10 the detailed organisation of planning, preparation and setting up the course is analysed. The course designer must insist that an arena party of not less than six strong people is available to him at times that suit his requirements. With such a team an enthusiast can do wonders with a simple set of fences by using his imagination and giving himself time to get things organised before the show. All the following items are comparatively inexpensive but make the arena a thing of beauty:

- Masses of fresh greenery that does not wilt (fir is best).
- Borrowed shrubs (in exchange for advertising).
- Boxes, tubs, pots of flowers.
- Christmas trees and planks with holes to hold them.
- Straw bales.
- Borrowed artificial grassmats.
- Rustic benches and wheelbarrows full of flowers.
- Wooden barrels (oil drums are awful).
- Freshly painted wooden cable drums.

These are the sort of items that a show can beg, borrow and steal to help the course designer to do a good job. He should not allow himself to be talked into doing the job with inadequate equipment for it is his reputation that is at stake.

PLANNING THE PROGRAMME

Since the course designer has to change his courses to fit into the programme, it is an obvious matter of good organisation for the committee to consider his problems when working out the timetable. The course designer must then understand the implications of the timetable and make his plans accordingly (see Chapter 10). Changes of course must be rapid for there is nothing that breaks the tension so completely as a prolonged pause whilst fences are moved.

I was once building courses in the United Arab Emirates where the programme for the final day went something like this:

Junior Grand Prix
Knock out pairs
6 bar jumping
Grand Prix

This looks like a really good programme for entertaining the crowd but it is a course designer's nightmare – especially as I had an arena party of only six people, most of whom had never done the job before and only one of whom spoke any English. However, we all got on splendidly with the work and with one another and battled through the heat of the day to keep within reasonable time. But it was not easy, and it is when a course designer is under pressure like that that mistakes can be made.

This would have been a perfectly acceptable programme if there were arena displays to fill in between classes while the course was changed and if there was a large and well-trained arena party.

When planning courses the course designer has conflicting problems – first, the necessity to make each course different and, second, to avoid delay.

Thus, in thinking about a change of course you must know in advance: what fences have to be moved or altered; when they are to be moved; and who is going to move each one. The answers depend on the size and experience of the arena party. Simplicity is the key. Clear thinking in the planning stage will ensure that dramatic changes can be made simply and easily.

JUDGES AND COURSE DESIGNERS

Under both International and National Rules the judges are responsible for all aspects of a competition, and this includes the course. The importance of a cordial relationship and one of mutual respect between judges and course designers cannot be too highly stressed. Judges must not forget that course designers at major shows are experts who have put a great deal of experience, time and energy into every course and take great pride in what they have created. It is a foolhardy judge who insists on alterations to the track without very good reasons indeed. If the course designer knows his job it is more likely that alterations will spoil the course rather than improve it. Judges should not forget when considering altering a course against the course designer's wishes, that they themselves have nothing to lose, whereas the course designer's reputation with riders and spectators is at risk whenever an unsatisfactory course is produced.

The course designer must accept the instructions of the judges and should always consider suggestions from them very carefully. Nevertheless, if the competition is not a success after alterations have been made, the relationship between course designer and judge can become a very unhappy one. The only circumstance in which judges *must* order the alteration of a fence is when it has been so constructed that it cannot be judged within the rules. This most often applies in connection with the meaning of the words 'vertical plane'. Judges and course designers must agree about this meaning and the latter must see that straight fences are constructed as the judges require.

When the judges inspect the course they can help the course designer in a number of ways. One is to check that all fences are correctly flagged, and another is to see that poles are resting freely in their cups and are not jammed against the supporting upright or wing. When working under pressure the course designer may not have inspected every fence with sufficient care and one does often find poles tightly jammed. This is both dangerous and unfair, for if a fence falls down it must be rebuilt to give the same resistance to a knock. It is not unknown for competitors to kick the base of the upright to tighten the poles when walking the course! All fences on the course must, as far as possible, give a uniform resistance to a blow from a horse.

To sum up these few important paragraphs: the ultimate responsibility under the rules rests upon the judges but the course designer is the expert whose opinion must be highly respected. Given acceptance of this, a co-operative situation is easy to obtain.

In Table 1 I have listed the jumping equipment and material required for constructing a championship course. This list is derived from one that I produced in South Africa as a guide to all the major show-holding bodies in that country that wished to qualify as a suitable venue for their national championships.

Photo 18 *Greg Best (USA) on the USET's Gem Twist at the Olympic Games in Seoul. This picture shows the marvellous presentation – here with dragons – of the beautiful fences.*

Table 1 *A list of equipment necessary for a show which includes a championship course.*

Equipment	For Course	Spare	Total	Remarks
1 Wings and/or uprights	58	10	68	Must be in pairs. For simplicity avoid many different colours. I recommend plain white and rustic.
2 **Poles**	50	10	60	Must be in sets of the same colour. I recommend 5 sets of 10 poles with 2 spare poles of each colour. Extra rustic (e.g. silver birch) poles are desirable.
3 **Planks**	6	2	8	Exactly the same length as the poles. Must have smooth edges. Must hang straight when placed in cups. 2 sets of 3 planks the same colour/pattern with one spare for each set.
4 **Gates**	2	2	4	Exactly the same length as the poles unless they are of a special design and will never be required to be used with a pole over the gate. They will be more versatile if the two pairs of gates are of different heights, e.g. 1 pair at 1.15 m (3 ft 9 ins) and 1 pair at 1.40 m (4 ft 6 ins). Each gate must have a spare.
5 **Cups** – for poles	100	20	120	Poles must roll freely in the cup which must not be deeper than (at most) half the diameter of the pole (FEI Regulations Article 208.4).
– for planks	12	4	16 }	Should be almost flat so that the plank will fall if hit with the same force as that required to dislodge a pole. It is best to paint the different types of cup in different colours for quick identification when building the course.
– for gates	4	4	8 }	
6 **Brush boxes**	5 sets	1 box for each set	5 + 5 boxes	1 set 1.10 m (3 ft 6 ins) 1 set 1.15 m (3 ft 9 ins) 1 set 1.20 m (4 ft) 1 set 1.30 m (4 ft 3 ins) Brush boxes need only be about 8 cm (3 ins) wide – this reduces weight and the amount of filling needed. They must fit exactly between the wings when the pole has been correctly placed on cups. 1 sloping set 40 cm (15 ins) for water jump if applicable.
7 **Walls** - full size	2	—	2	Capable of going to 1.80 m (6 ft) or 2.30 m (7 ft 6 ins) if needed for a Puissance competition. Pillars, higher than the wall at maximum height, are necessary. Walls must fit exactly between wings under a pole so that they can be used with poles as a filler if required.
– small walls	2	—	2	For fillers. Capable of being set at heights from 0.90–1.20 m (3–4 ft). Must fit exactly under poles.

Equipment	For Course	Spare	Total	Remarks
8 Picket fences	9	3	12	Approximately 30 cm (1 ft) high. Must have rounded tops. Ideal for providing strong attractive groundline to many fences. 3 pickets must exactly fit under poles.

9 Hurdles	3 sets	1 for each set	3 + 3 hurdles	Painted 1 set 1.10 m (3 ft 6 ins)
				          1 set 1.20 m (4 ft)
				          1 set 1.30 m (4 ft 3 ins)
				Each set of three hurdles must fit exactly under poles.

	2 sets	2 hurdles	2 + 2 hurdles	Rustic 1 set 1.10 m (3 ft 6 ins) 1 set 1.20 m (4 ft) These are self-supporting and do not need to hang in cups.
10 Wooden barrels	2 rows	—	2	If available. If placed on their side must be wedged to prevent them rolling.
11 Other fillers	6 sets	As appropriate	As appropriate	Must fit exactly under poles. Examples are benches, balustrades, coops, flower boxes, straw bales.
12 Shrubs	34 large	—	34	About 1.50 m (5 ft) tall to decorate wings. In plastic or wooden tubs.
	30 small	—	30	About 1 m (3 ft 3 ins) tall to go into the building of the actual fence.
13 Start and finish signs	—	—	—	Self-supporting.
Jump numbers	2 sets Also 3 × 'A', 3 × 'B' and 3 × 'C' for combinations	—	—	Numbers 1–17. Each set a different colour. Self-supporting.
14 Jump flags	30 pairs	—	—	1 red/1 white per pair. Must be easily stuck into ground. If made of wood or metal they must not be pointed (to avoid accidents). Or can be attached to a short pole that fits into a holder on the wing.

4 ◇ *Simple Principles*

So far I have defined our objectives, studied some of the technicalities relating to how a horse jumps and outlined the role of the course designer at a show. In this chapter I have listed some simple principles and guidelines. Many of these ideas are also explored later in the book.

WHAT TO DO

Keep the line between the fences as simple as possible.
A simple track to be followed encourages flowing, bold, rhythmical jumping that is attractive to watch and a pleasure to ride. But try and use imagination to make the line more interesting than just a figure of eight. Avoid square corners (Figs 12 and 13).

Think always of the approach to the fence.
The approach is by far the most important phase of a horse's jump. Provided he arrives at the point of take-off in balance and with impulsion nothing much can go wrong. Riders must be given the opportunity to decide their own approach path, and ample room to get at a fence. In a jump-off or a timed competition the rider who manages to take the shortest track will score but it is better that he decides this for himself rather than have his path dictated to him by the course designer. This is more clearly seen by reference to Fig. 10.

In Fig. 10 the options are left open and skill is at a premium. I have shown the possible location of a fence that is to be used earlier, or later, in the course and which could be carefully sited to give competitors the choice of which side to go when riding against the clock.

Vary fences between uprights, parallels and staircase fences.
It is always worthwhile checking to see that your course contains a mixture of all three types of fence – not forgetting the occasional use of a narrow fence or stile. When you have decided your jump-off course check again to make sure that you still have a proper mixture of fences.

Course to work to a climax.
As discussed in Chapter 1.

Encourage bold jumping into a line of fences or a combination.
A fair approach to an inviting fence will help to produce really good jumping.

Be consistent in size throughout the course.
It is disconcerting for horse and rider if some fences are much smaller than others. Even the first fence should not be a give-away. One quite often sees good horses refuse the very easy first fence whereas something more testing serves notice on competitors that there is work ahead. A very good rule for riders is: always ride the first fence of a course as if it is five foot high.

Distribute fences evenly around the arena.
This for two reasons: first, the arena looks very wrong if most fences are huddled together in one area; second, spectators must all get a fair view of what is going on. The closer they are to a fence the greater their feeling of involvement. Check your jump-off course too, especially if fences not needed in the jump-off are taken out, to ensure that it is well distributed. Always bear in mind the position of the main area of spectator seating.

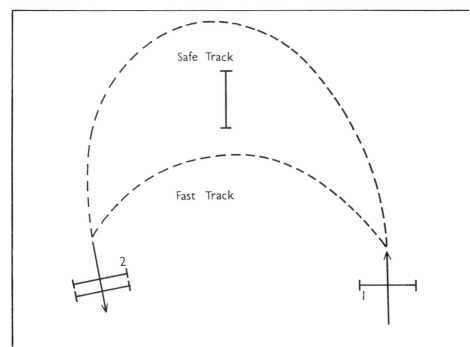

Fig. 10 *Here the options are left open and skill is at a premium. I have shown the possible location of another fence which could be carefully sited so that a competitor has the choice of which side to go when riding against the clock.*

Include an absolute minimum of one change of direction.
Most good courses contain not less than two changes of direction. A trained show jumper must be equally happy on either rein and must change automatically. Make sure that your jump-off course also has changes of rein. In a speed class several changes should be included but they must not be such that the good rider cannot maintain the flow and rhythm of his round. A good speed course, or one for a jump-off, should test a horse's ability both to turn and to gallop.

Avoid trick fences.
Never forget that the object of any course design is to produce good jumping. It is a poor course designer who has to resort to an 'eliminator' to produce a result. In a good course faults are evenly distributed between all the fences; if one fence causes most of the faults it is a bad fence.

Fences to give uniform resistance to a blow.
If you are provided with one fence that falls too easily, do not use it. Check that the right cups are used with the appropriate material. Planks and gates need different fittings from poles. Each different type of cup should be painted a different colour for quick identification.

Consider colour.
Your fences will include many different colours. Plan your use of colour to suit your own taste but do not just allow a chaotic mixture. Most course designers use only one set of colours (for example red and white) in a combination but this may sometimes look puzzling to horse and rider. Always check the background to ensure that a fence does not merge into it and become difficult to define.

Check the position of the afternoon sun.
If jumping is to take place when the sun is low, take great care that fences jumped into the sun are clearly defined.

WHAT NOT TO DO

Don't try to be too clever.
It is always tempting to try to achieve something new and unusual. Always bear in mind that you have a great responsibility for the safety of horse and rider. As I have already written, it is simplicity that generally produces the best course and original ideas should be implemented with care and discretion.

Don't start novice horses away from the entrance.
The horse is a gregarious animal and among his original sins is a desire to return to his fellows. Therefore you can ask for greater effort going towards home and must encourage him with easy jumps away from the gate. A novice will also take a longer stride towards, and a shorter stride away from, the entrance to the arena.

Don't put an awkward turn or difficult fence away from the entrance.
This for the same reasons given in the previous paragraph. In the Hamburg Derby
Course there is a double of banks right across the entrance which is through a
tunnel beneath the judges' tower. It is surprising how many horses, even of
international standard, show a distinct desire to leave the arena at this juncture
(see Fig. 11).

This may sound very obvious but it is all part of the course designer's armoury
to know how a horse thinks and, having understood, to build accordingly.

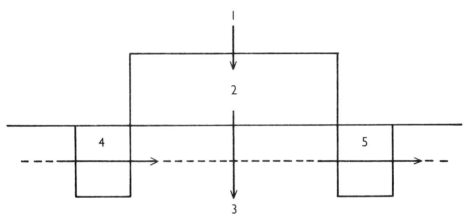

Fig. 11 *Double of banks at Hamburg:*
1 = *Collecting ring*
2 = *Judges' tower*
3 = *Entrance*
4 = *Bank A*
5 = *Bank B*

Don't break the rhythm of the course.
I remember being taught by H. H. Brinkman who said: 'Put your horse into a
rhythm before you go through the start and keep that rhythm until you pass the
finish.' Watch David Broome if you want to see that precept carried out to
perfection.

Fig. 12 was a course produced for part of a seminar I was running in Rhodesia
(now Zimbabwe) in 1977. The designer thought that it contained one change of
direction. We put it up and sent some novice horses around it in order to prove
that, although it might have looked all right on paper, in practice it produced seven
changes of leg shown by the figures in circles (Fig. 13). Over a track like that it was
impossible for an inexperienced horse to maintain any sort of rhythm at all.

In Fig. 12 it looks at least credible that this track would contain only one change
of direction, at fence 2. By filling in the line taken by almost all novice horses we
find seven changes of leg (Fig. 13).

This shows, again, how vital it is that the course designer understands what will

Fig. 12

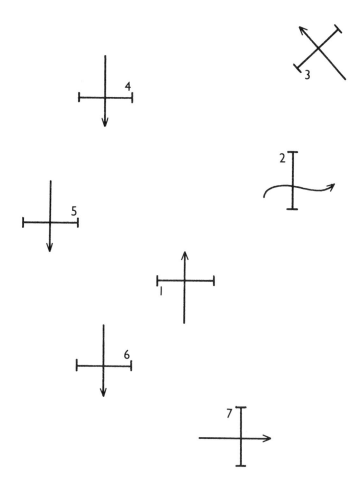

Figs 12 and 13   *In Fig. 12 it looks at least credible that this was a track containing only one change of direction, at fence 2. By filling in the line taken by almost all novice horses (Fig. 13) we find seven changes (shown by the figures in the circles). This shows, again, how vital it is that the course designer understands what will actually happen over his course in real life. It also highlights the great difference between drawing on paper and building the course on the ground. The skill lies in knowing how the horses for whom you have built will perform and react over the test that has been set.*

Note: Fences 6 and 7 show what is meant by a square corner. They do not ride well.

Fig. 13

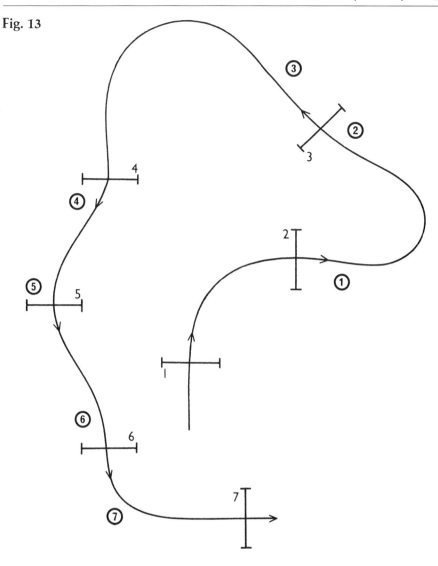

actually happen over his course in real life. It also highlights the great difference between drawing some marks on paper and putting up an actual course. The skill lies in knowing how the horses for whom you have built will perform and react.

The simple principles that have been set out in this chapter should be in the forefront of a course designer's mind when he is planning courses. Similarly, a beginner can use each one as a question:

- 'Is the track simple?'
- 'Are all the approaches fair?'

- 'Have I got a good mixture of fences?'
- 'What about my jump-off?'
- 'Have I got changes of direction?', etc. – and if he checks through each one, he should not go far wrong.

The last thing that is wanted is for everyone to build courses exactly the same. However, there are distinct basic principles that must be agreed by us all. Within this framework, an individual course designer's signature on his finished arena is as clear and as personal as that of a painter on his canvas.

To lay down the law might be not only offensive to excellent course designers with different views, but may also tend to stifle the flowering of that essential individual genius and style which, when present, makes show jumping so much more interesting.

5 ◇ *The Course*

We have already decided that there are two sorts of show jumping, one for spectators and one for riders. The question the course designer must ask is, 'Who am I building for?' Is it riders, horses or spectators? So far all our theories have been concerned with the physical and mental attributes of the horse. Since our first objective was 'to produce an exciting event for spectators' it is our paying public that command our first responsibility.

Fortunately there need be no conflict of interest because if you produce a competition that thrills and delights the crowd, you will certainly have a very satisfied bunch of competitors. But you must keep this objective in mind and not just become a technician whose purpose is to match your own skills against the physical capabilities of the horse and the excellence of the rider. This especially applies in 'fun' classes, which are often spoiled as entertainment by the fences being too big. I am thinking about competitions like the Jigsaw Pairs and various forms of Take Your Own Line where speed is of the essence and the crowd want to see horses really having a go. I am *not* suggesting that the fences should be ridiculously small – but keep in mind that three inches means nothing to spectators but can make all the difference in the way riders will tackle the course.

DERBIES AND CLEAR ROUNDS

Each course must suit the type of class for which it is designed and these are of tremendous variety. Each class demands special thought to produce the right answer that will meet all objectives.

There is nothing more calculated to stop a course designer in his tracks than to be asked to set up a 'Derby' course. For standard competitions and championships I believe that six to eight clears is an ideal number. A Derby course, however, is ridden over a greater distance and over more and bigger obstacles than any other and it is not really very desirable to have to go to a jump-off. The effort required over one such round is as much as should be asked of any horse on one day. On the other hand, a competition without a clear round can be very anti-climactic. It follows, therefore, that in a Derby the perfect solution to aim for is just one clear round.

The problem of how to achieve this is something which gives much thought. It is a very salutary exercise and one that may cause the designer to reconsider all his ideas in some detail. This is a good thing because over a long period of time there is a danger of becoming complacent and of setting courses without really thinking what he is doing. His courses may develop a predictable sameness that is boring to spectators and uninteresting for competitors. So an invitation to build for a Derby and to try for just one clear round has a profound effect on one's thinking.

The first thing that struck me, when I was asked to build a Derby course for the first time at the 1975 Rothman's Derby in Johannesburg, was the importance of cutting out all wasted fences; to make every obstacle one that would cause a rider who lost concentration a problem. Secondly, it is usual for Derby courses to have a number of special fences of which the Devil's Dyke and the planks after the bank claim the greatest number of victims, and I wondered how many clear rounds there would be if one discounted faults incurred at these two obstacles. My approach to the Derby, therefore, was to increase the accuracy required for every fence on the course and to decrease the severity of the Devil's Dyke, my thinking based on the agreed principle of course building that, if one fence causes a majority of the faults, it is a bad one.

Following this train of thought and applying it to more conventional competitions produces some interesting ideas which, while not necessarily new, ought to improve all one's courses from the point of view of spectators as well as demanding better and more thoughtful riding – without producing bad rounds, eliminations and unhappy horses or riders.

I have included here the design for the Johannesburg Derby (see Fig. 14). This course was to produce only eight clear rounds in as many years. This was nothing compared to Pam Carruthers' record in producing exactly twenty-one clear rounds in her first twenty-one years at Hickstead.

DISTANCE

It is worth thinking about how long a horse should be on the track. Clearly it is difficult to build short courses in very big arenas but the sooner a competition can reach the jump-off stage the more exciting it is going to be. Consider the average course and think how many 'give-away' fences we all tend to include that really serve no purpose at all except to get a horse from A to B. But they do unnecessarily increase the strain on horses whose season is ever longer and who are asked to jump day after day, often with only travelling time between.

I believe that 75 seconds is as long as a horse should be expected to take to jump a course and that 10 to 11 fences – provided they are the right ones – is about an ideal number. In these circumstances each fence must be expected to take its toll in faults while spectators' attention is held all the time and a climax is reached more quickly. Fewer fences means that a higher standard of presentation can be achieved, as well as reducing the workload on the arena party, giving a quicker setting up time as an added bonus.

If you put these ingredients together successfully, you will end up with a course that fulfils the criteria for excellence:

- The competition is kept to as short a duration as is reasonably possible and ends with excitement at a high pitch.
- All horses are encouraged to give their best and produce sparkling performances, so that even those with faults are rewarded with a sense of achievement.
- Faults are evenly spread over the course and occur whenever a rider loses concentration.
- The best horses and riders in the competition head the line-up at the end.

THE JUMP-OFF

A jump-off must include changes of direction. Very well. The difficulty is that after planning what looks like a super track for the first round, it is sometimes difficult to find a good jump-off course.

In order to get a good track for the jump-off, it is quite all right to put the fences in a different order from that used in the first round. This is an accepted practice and greatly helps to work out an ideal solution.

The course designer must keep the time judge in mind whenever designing a jump-off course. An alteration in the position of the electric timing gear between rounds of a competition may be required and the pause that takes place while the timing is moved will certainly break the tension in the crowd, which could spoil the competition. If possible the timing should not have to be moved and the jump-off track should be planned accordingly.

The jump-off is the climax to the competition. A marvellous first round can be spoiled by an ill-planned jump-off course. The questions that stem from the general principles in Chapter 4 must be used to provide a yardstick to assess the jump-off so as to be sure of ending each competition on a high note of excitement.

Do not make up your mind about the size of fences for the jump-off too soon. Your decision should depend on how well the horses have jumped in the first round and how many have gone clear. If the fences are already very demanding and if the horses have a heavy programme ahead, it is perfectly acceptable (and often very sensible) not to raise them at all.

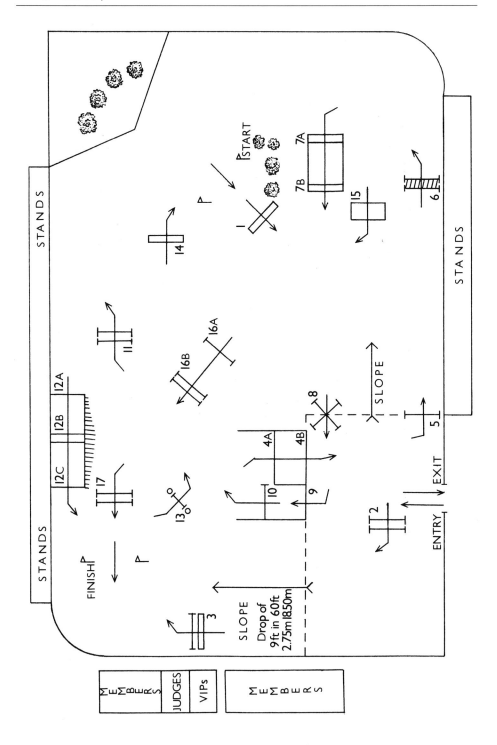

Fence	Description	Height	Spread	Distance	Remarks
1	Permanent stone wall	1.40 m (4 ft 6 ins)	—	—	
2	Parallel over brush. Green/white	1.40 m × 1.40 m (4 ft 6 ins × 4 ft 6 ins)	1.50 m (5 ft)	—	
3	Liverpool over dry ditch. Orange/White	0.30 m/1.50 m (1–4 ft)	1.50 m (5 ft)	—	Flower boxes under front pole
4A	Step up with white pole	—	—	—	Permanent obstacle
4B	Step up with white pole	—	—	—	Permanent obstacle
5	Garden balustrade	1.45 m (4 ft 9 ins)	—	—	At top of slope
6	Parallel over natural hedge	1.45 m × 1.45 m (4 ft 9 ins × 4 ft 9 ins)	1.80 m (6 ft)	—	
7A	Bank and pole and ditch on to platform	1.45 m (4 ft 9 ins)	—	—	Permanent obstacle
7B	Ditch, bank and pole off platform	1.45 m (4 ft 9 ins)	—	—	Permanent obstacle
8	Star fence. White	1.40 m (4 ft 6 ins)	—	—	At top of sharp rise
9	Vertical drop Derby bank	2.60 m (8 ft 6 ins)	—	—	Permanent obstacle
10	Planks. Green/white	1.50 m (5 ft)	—	10 m (33 ft)	
11	Parallel over hedge	1.50 m (5 ft)	1.7 cm (5 ft 7 ins)	—	
12A	Into Devil's Dyke	1.40 m (4 ft 6 ins)	—	—	
12B	Poles over water	1.40 m (4 ft 6 ins)	—	—	} Permanent obstacle
12C	Out of Devil's Dyke	1.40 m (4 ft 6 ins)	—	—	
13	Picnic table with white poles	1.50 m (5 ft)	—	—	Between 2 over-hanging poplar trees
14	Grey wall	1.60 m (5 ft 3 ins)	—	—	
15	Water	—	4.60 m (15 ft)	—	White plank for take-off
16A	White gate	1.45 m (4 ft 6 ins)	—	—	
16B	Parallel white gate and pole	1.45 m × 1.50 m (4 ft 6 ins × 5 ft)	1.50 m (5 ft)	7.60 m (25 ft)	
17	Rustic parallel	1.50 m × 1.50 m (5 ft × 5 ft)	1.80 m (6 ft)	—	

Fig. 14 *The course for the Rothmans Derby, held at the Inanda Club, Johannesburg, 1977.*
Table A. Article 238.1.C.
Speed: 400 m/min (435 yds/min)
Distance: 1000 m (1090 yds)
This course achieved only eight clear rounds in as many years.

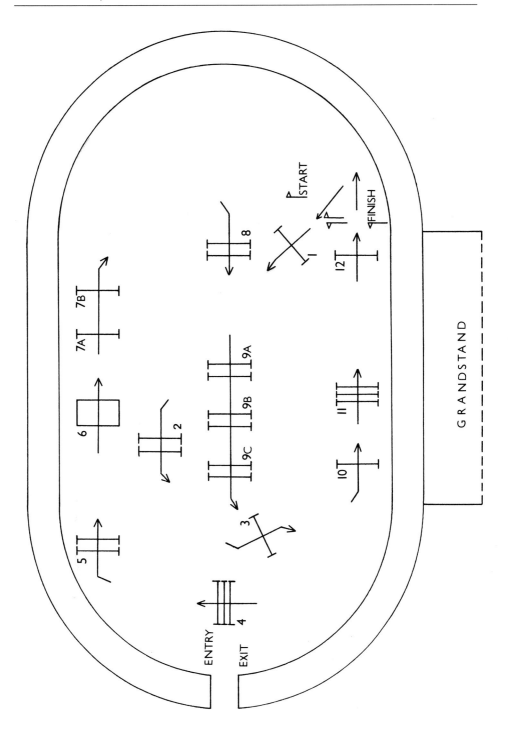

Fence	Description	Height	Spread	Distance	Remarks
1	White wall fence and poles spread	1.30 m (4 ft 3 ins)	1.40 m (4 ft 6 ins)	—	—
2	Rustic parallel over straw bales	1.40 m (4 ft 6 ins)	1.50 m (5 ft)	—	—
3	Red pillars and red/white poles upright full width	1.45 m (4 ft 9 ins)	—	—	Check siting as option from 9C–10 in jump-off
4	Triple bar poles, shrubs, flowers	1.20 m/1.45 m (4 ft–4 ft 9 ins)	1.80 m (6 ft)	—	—
5	Wall with pillars	1.50 m (5 ft)	—	—	—
6	Water, low sloping brush only in front	—	4.60 m (15 ft)	26.50 m (87 ft)	—
7A	Vertical planks and poles	1.40 m (4 ft 6 ins)	—	23 m (75 ft)	—
7B	Vertical planks and poles	1.45 m (4 ft 9 ins)	—	7.90 m (26 ft)	—
8	Spread of brush and poles behind yellow/white	1.40 m (4 ft 6 ins)	—	—	—
9A	Parallel of brush and green poles	1.40/1.45 m (4 ft 6 ins/4 ft 9 ins)	1.40 m (4 ft 6 ins)	29.50 m (98 ft)	—
9B	Parallel of brush and orange/white poles	1.45 m (4 ft 9 ins)	1.50 m (5 ft)	7.80 m (25 ft 6 ins)	—
9C	Parallel of brush of green/white poles	1.45 m (4 ft 9 ins)	1.60 m (5 ft 3 ins)	7.60 m (25 ft)	—
10	Gates and stone pillars	1.45 m (4 ft 9 ins)	—	—	—
11	Triple bar	1.20 m–1.50 m (4–5 ft)	1.80 m (6 ft)	14.50 m (48 ft)	—
12	V fence, upright, full width	1.50 m (5 ft)	—	more than 30 m (100 ft)	—

Fig. 15 *The course for the Rand Show, Johannesburg, CSI 1977. The White Horse Whisky Championship course. Table A. Article 238.1.*
Speed: 400 m/min (435 yds/min)
Distance: 535 m (585 yds)
Jump-off fences: 1, 7B, 9, 10, 11, 12
Distance: 330 m (360 yds).

6 ◈ Tests, Problems and Related Distances

Every fence in a course must have a purpose and must demand concentration from rider and horse. Ideally, faults in any competition must be evenly distributed around the course. In setting tests for horses and riders it is necessary to study distances between fences, both in and out of combination, and factors that affect length of stride and impulsion, and the course designer must understand the instinctive reaction that a horse will produce under a given set of circumstances.

FENCES WHICH ARE SIMILAR

Basically the average horse's normal stride at canter at speeds between 320 m (350 yds) and 415 m (450 yds) per minute can be taken as 3.50 m (12 ft) long.

Since we have already discovered that the distance a horse covers over a fence is approximately 3.50 m (12 ft) plus the width of the fence (see Chapter 2), it follows that similar fences should be set at 3.50 m (12 ft) intervals if the horse is to meet them in his stride.

Thus, for three strides between similar fences a distance of 14.50 m (48 ft) should be ideal. This is shown in Figs. 16 and 17 and the same principle applies, as:

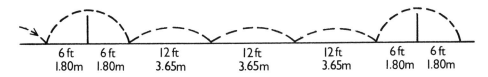

| 6 ft | 6 ft | 12 ft | 12 ft | 12 ft | 6 ft | 6 ft |
| 1.80m | 1.80m | 3.65m | 3.65m | 3.65m | 1.80m | 1.80m |

Fig. 16 *Upright to upright.*

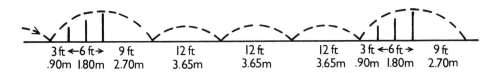

| 3 ft ←6 ft→ | 9 ft | 12 ft | 12 ft | 12 ft | 3 ft ←6 ft→ | 9 ft |
| .90m 1.80m | 2.70m | 3.65m | 3.65m | 3.65m | .90m 1.80m | 2.70m |

Fig. 17 *Triple bar to triple bar.*

- For four strides between similar fences a distance of 18 m (60 ft).
- For five strides between similar fences a distance of 21.50 m (72 ft).
- For six strides between similar fences a distance of 25 m (84 ft).

The greater the distance, the less critical it becomes.

Now we come to an anomaly because if you take this principle and try to apply it to fences less than three strides apart you will come up with a distance that is too short. The reason is that horse and rider, seeing fences very close together ahead, increase their powerful forward movement (impulsion) so as to have sufficient energy to jump the second and third parts of the combination.

Thus, rather than 7.30 m (24 ft) or 10.90 m (36 ft) in a double of similar fences I would use 7.60 m (25 ft) or 11.20 m (37 ft), subject to the other factors that are discussed below.

The explanation of why the distance between two similar fences remains constant is clearly demonstrated in Figures 18, 19, and 20. This follows on from our analysis of the jump made by the horse over upright, parallel and spread fences in Chapter 2 (see Figs. 1, 2 and 3).

In Fig. 18 the distance A to B equals that of B to C, which equals that of D to E and of E to F. The overall distance between B and E being 7.60 m (25 ft).

In Fig. 19, C to D is greater than E to F. The horse will land further out from

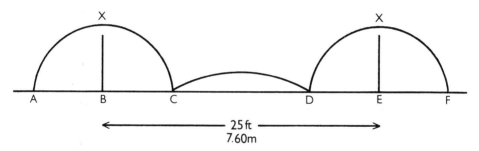

Fig. 18   *Upright to upright. AB = BC = DE = EF ≃ 1.80 m (6 ft).*

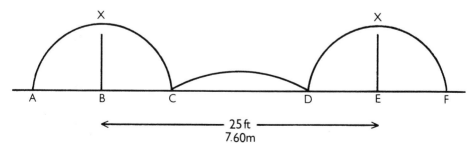

Fig. 19   *Parallel to parallel. AB = EF. CD is greater than EF. The horse lands further out from the first fence, so its single stride brings it closer to the second, which is the right place to take off at a parallel.*

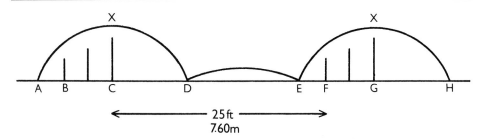

Fig. 20 *Staircase to staircase. AB = EF. CD is much greater than EF. This is an extension of what happens between two parallels. The far out landing over the first fence, followed by one stride, brings the horse right into the base of the second from where it can easily tackle this triple bar. It is essential to understand why the distance (7.60 m/25 ft) between any two fences with a similar profile always remains constant.*

the first fence, so that its single stride brings it closer to the base of the second – which is the right place to take off at a parallel.

In Fig. 20, C to D is *much* greater than E to F. This is an extension of what happens between two parallels. The far out landing over the first fence followed by one stride brings the horse right into the base of the second fence, from where it can easily tackle this triple bar.

FENCES THAT ARE NOT ALIKE

Now let us look at distances between fences that are not alike. Everyone knows that the distance from a spread to an upright should be longer than the standard and that the distance from an upright to a spread fence should be shorter. These two statements are illustrated in more detail in Figs. 21 and 22. When the aspiring course designer has mastered these simple principles he is on the way to building lovely, jumpable and interesting courses – and he will do so with confidence because he understands the reasons for what he is doing.

In Fig. 21 if you substituted a 1.80 m (6 ft) wide triple bar for the second part of this double at the same distance of 8.20 m (27 ft) it is clear that you would be asking for trouble. You would be expecting the horse to stand off 2 m (6 ft 6 ins) at a triple bar, reach the top of his flight 3.80 m (12 ft 6 ins) from take-off and therefore to cover a distance from take-off to landing of 7.60 m (25 ft) – only .65 m (2 ft 2 ins) short of the world long-jump record! Note, too, for future reference, the steep angle of descent over the upright fence and the flatter parabola over the spread fence.

Photos 19–24 *Staircase to upright (8.20 m/27 ft). The distances, shown by the white lines on the grass, are as given in Fig. 21. This is a lovely combination for spectators when looked at from the side. Even with the fences only at 1.20 m (4 ft) you can see the magnificence of the jump at the second element.*

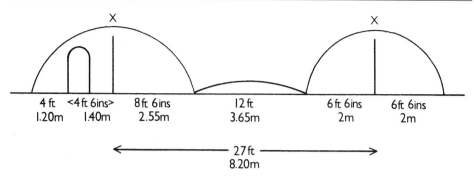

Fig. 21 *Staircase to upright.*

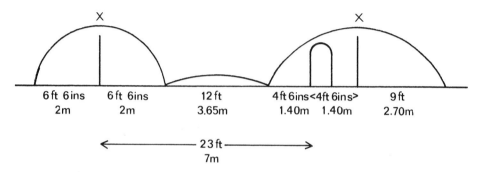

Fig. 22 *Upright to staircase.*

Looking at Fig. 22 we can see that if you substituted a 1.45 m (4 ft 9 ins) upright for the second part of this double at the same distance of 7 m (23 ft) it is clear that the distance would be almost impossibly short. It would certainly necessitate some severe hooking up by the rider and kill all rhythm and flow over the course.

From these two extremes we can now deduce a table of easy distances (see Fig. 23) for horses in combinations.

Using this information as a basis for setting distances in double and treble combinations should work out very well in normal conditions. The many variable factors that affect distance are discussed later in this chapter but the following general principles should be borne in mind:

- Use fair, easy distances in all but advanced competitions, also at the beginning of a show.
- For medium classes it is better to have big fences in combinations set at easy distances than smaller fences at awkward ones.

Photos 25–30 *Upright to staircase. The distances, shown by the white lines on the grass, are exactly as given in Fig. 22. Charles and Alfoxton demonstrate why the figures always work out correctly.*

		SECOND FENCE		
		Upright	Parallel	Staircase
FIRST FENCE	Upright	7.60 m (25 ft)	7.30 m (24 ft)	7 m (23 ft)
	Parallel	7.90 m (26 ft)	7.60 m (25 ft)	7.30 m (24 ft)
	Staircase	8.20 m (27 ft)	7.90 m (26 ft)	7.60 m (25 ft)

Fig. 23 *Table of easy distances in combinations, for horses. To convert the distance to two strides, add 3.30 m (11 ft).*

- Except in very demanding courses let the first fence of a treble invite horses to jump in boldly to encourage confident jumping.
- When varying the distances be consistent. Do not in one combination have a short distance followed by a long one or vice versa (except in very high class competitions).
- If your treble combination is used in the jump-off and comes immediately after a very sharp turn, do not use a wide spread as the second element. This can result in horrifying crashes if a competitor comes in too sharply and/or slips on take-off.

For all fences set at related distances, up to 25 m (84 ft), there are several variable factors that must be taken into account. They include:

- The nature of the obstacles.
- The likely impulsion of a horse at any point.
- The state of the going.
- Location of obstacles, especially in relation to the exit gate.

Let us discuss each of these factors in a little more detail under their respective headings.

THE OBSTACLES

I well remember the late Colonel Jack Talbot Ponsonby saying that it is mathematically impossible for a horse to be more than half a stride wrong at any fence. If you think about it this is absolutely true. If he is more than half a stride away from the ideal point of take-off, he will be obliged to put in a short stride and either jump or refuse. It is highly unlikely that any horse would be foolhardy enough to attempt a jump from more than half a stride plus the normal distance from take-off to the base of the fence. (This would, on average, total 3.60 m (12 ft).)

In setting up fences at related distances there are two ways in which you can increase the difficulty of your test. One is to set the fences at awkward distances and the other is to let the nature of the fences do the job for you.

The placing of fences at awkward distances tends to produce unattractive jumping and loss of rhythm if taken to extremes (the extreme is half a stride). But there is nothing wrong with asking a horse to lengthen or shorten stride between two fences provided such a test is not taken to excess.

Bear in mind that it is easier to jump a vertical fence off a short stride than a long one, and easier to jump a wide, staircase type fence off a lengthening stride than when shortening. Set your test accordingly, deciding whether you want a very stiff test (such as jumping a vertical fence off a long stride), a moderately difficult test (such as asking for some degree of lengthening into a staircase fence), or to make it as easy as possible by using a conventional distance, multiples of 3.50 m (12 ft).

Faults that take place at one fence may well have started to happen at the fence before, or even earlier, especially where they are set at related distances. A commonly used, and excellent, test is to follow an inviting staircase type fence after three or four strides by a stiff vertical. At the former, a horse is encouraged to travel on, give a big jump and come out of the fence with a long, powerful stride that must be controlled before taking off at the latter. In this case a small shortening of the conventional distance of, for example, 14.50 m (48 ft) or 18 m (60 ft), will greatly increase the severity of the test as, indeed, will a lengthening of the distance. This is just one of very many permutations that can be worked out depending on the nature of obstacles set at related distances.

The good course designer will work out the distances he wants to use related to the type of fence he is proposing to build. It is well worth taking a lot of trouble to get just the test you want and so produce interesting and attractive jumping. It is also well worth competitors understanding these principles so that they can 'read a course' correctly when they walk around before the competition. The educated rider can save a lot of faults and last-minute adjustments in the horse's stride by getting inside the mind of the designer before riding the course.

IMPULSION

The shape of the horse's jump follows the shape of the fence. The parabola described is steeper over an upright fence than over a staircase. (Clearly a flat, long trajectory over a vertical is a sure way of collecting faults.) The stride after landing steeply is bound to be shorter than after a shallower jump.

Impulsion is the powerful, forward moving, controlled energy that the horse has available for making the great physical effort needed for a jump. This energy must be maintained right up to the moment of take-off, especially during a process of lengthening or shortening stride. The course designer must carefully consider how much or how little impulsion a horse is likely to have available as a result of the tests he has set. The more impulsion that is lost, the more difficulty there will be in clearing a closely related spread fence, especially if the stride or strides towards it have to be longer than normal.

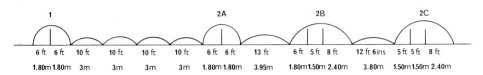

Fig. 24 *Four strides from 1 to 2A.*

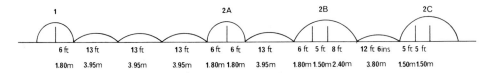

Fig. 25 *Three strides from 1 to 2A.*

Figs 24–25 *Two theoretical stride arrangements over this very difficult test. A check back to the distances and principles explained in this chapter will show how severe this test was and why no one succeeded in jumping it clear.*

Fence 1, 1.50 m (5 ft) upright of 0.05 m (2 ins) diameter poles
Fence 2A, 1.45 m (4 ft 9 ins) upright poles
Fence 2B, 1.50 m (5 ft) parallel
Fence 2C, 1.50 m (5 ft) parallel
Distances: 1–2A = 15.50 m (51 ft)
*   2A–2B = 7.60 m (25 ft)*
*   2B–2C = 7.80 m (25 ft 6 ins).*

I watched a very clear demonstration of this over a very big track a few years ago. The test is shown in Figs 24–25. No one cleared it, although there were some valiant attempts. I did not have the opportunity accurately to measure the distances between the fences but I have added distances that would produce the same result and the same test.

It is a design that only a very bold and experienced course designer, who was building for great horses, would attempt – especially when, as in this case, the course was built on a slight uphill slope. This was a very cunning test, and worth analysing for the lessons to be learned from its design. The first fence was an upright of lightweight poles that fell very easy. Riders had the choice of taking the risk and going into it very strongly, which put them into a reasonable position for tackling the combination, or going in carefully to clear the fence, but needing a very athletic and clever horse to have a hope over what was still to come.

If they selected to go in boldly over the lead-in fence, they were still faced with three long strides into another formidable upright at the beginning of the combination. Of those who opted for this approach all had one or both of the uprights down, but most cleared the two big parallels.

Most of those who chose to go in carefully and try for four strides were clear over the two uprights. However, they landed very steeply over the first part of the combination and took a short stride, which put them too far off the first of the two big parallels. They then landed with practically no forward movement, to be faced with a very long stride into a huge parallel which none of them succeeded in clearing.

In fact only one horse cleared the whole test after taking four strides between the two vertical fences. But on landing over the first parallel in what seemed a no-hope situation, the horse uncoiled a leap of such fantastic power to clear the last that the rider was unseated to the great disappointment of the crowd.

A combination of an upright and two parallels is probably the most difficult of all and to precede it by another upright is to set a very severe test indeed. I have quoted this example to illustrate how the nature of the fences and their relationship in distance has a dramatic effect on the horse's ability to jump them clear. Any two of these fences would have given few problems to the high-class field involved; any three of them would undoubtedly have yielded plenty of clear rounds, but the diabolically clever setting of all four was indeed a difficult test to solve. Had the designer decided to offer two strides between any two elements of the combination, he would have lessened the severity of the test and allowed horse and rider more opportunity to recover lost impulsion. As it was, it was a fascinating test from which a great deal of information could be deduced. By the criteria that we have set, though, it proved in the event to be just too demanding.

It is fair enough to ask for a big stand-off at a vertical fence but courting disaster to do so at a parallel or spread.

THE GOING

It goes without saying that the state of the going affects the length of a horse's stride as well as his ability to get off the ground with sufficient power to clear large obstacles. Having worked both in Britain and in Southern Africa I am convinced that firm ground is much less damaging to a horse's legs than soft, muddy ground.

But differences in going are amazing and not easy to judge in advance. Some ground may appear good, but ride very dead; other turf, even after a soaking, can retain its springy quality.

Old turf on a light sandy loam soil cannot be beaten. I am also convinced that organic fertilisers improve the riding quality of an arena more effectively than the use of artificial fertilisers. It is generally accepted today that it is important to leave plenty of cover on a showground and I like to see around 8 cm (3 ins) of grass over the arena.

The most important thing is that the going should not be slippery, and it is in this respect that sandy soils are so good. If you do have a heavy loam or clay, the worst thing you can do is to water just before or during the show. The water does not drain, leaving a layer of slippery mud between the grass on top and the baked clay only an inch or so below.

If you have the problem of hard ground the answer is to flood it three days before the show so that even if a crust forms during the interval it is soft

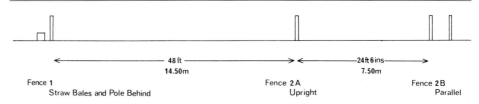

Fig. 26 *A simple test at an indoor show.*

underneath and the 'bone' has been taken out of it.

The greatest difficulty comes from ground that changes during a competition. I was building a course at an indoor show and set as the first two fences what was a simple test (see Fig. 26).

All went exactly according to plan with three easy strides between Fences 1 and 2A for the first half of the large field engaged in the contest.

Gradually the ground in front of Fence 1 broke up and became deeper and deeper until the unfortunate competitors had to ride hard for three good strides or hook up for four. Most of them managed it without desperate difficulty since the fences were not large but, for those who went later, the rhythm of their rounds, which was perfect at the start of the competition, was badly disrupted.

Dramatic changes in going like this are unlikely to confront the course designer outdoors. If, after rain, the going becomes heavy and holding not only should the distance between closely related fences be shortened, but also the size of the fences should be reduced – especially the width of spread fences, since the clinging mud prevents the horse from getting smoothly and powerfully off the ground.

If the ground is hard, and water is not available, sand, shavings or peat must be laid for take-off and landings. Don't forget that a horse takes off and lands well out from the fence and your soft material must be put in the right place. Material placed in front of a fence must extend far enough out so that it does not create a false take-off line. For the same reason, if it is used in the arena, it must also be put down in the warming-up area so that competitors can get used to it. Material placed beyond a fence need only start about 1.50 m (5 ft) from the back of the fence.

LOCATION OF OBSTACLES

The effect of the siting of fences on stride, and the importance of location generally has been dealt with in Chapter 4.

It used to be all the rage among course designers to set courses that consisted almost entirely of a number of lines of fences all related by stride. It gave a wonderful feeling of power to dictate to riders exactly how every fence must be jumped and how many strides must be taken between each! Then came a period when this became unfashionable and courses tended to become rather long and strung out.

Today I think a happy medium prevails as riders are rightly asked to be able both to ride fences at related distances and individual obstacles. I love to give competitors a good long run in to a big parallel or a big upright fence and both these tests demand a lot of skill. So, do not be rigid in your thinking and planning – a good show jumper can cope with any kind of test provided it is fair and the designer knows what he is doing. In indoor arenas courses almost inevitably consist of lines of related fences. Building indoors is discussed later.

It cannot be too strongly emphasised that the course designer must always be aware, when designing a course, of the location of the entry and exit gate. Not only is this gate a temptation to horses to nap towards it, but it also plays an important part in keeping the competition to time. You must site your first and last fences to cause the minimum delay between rounds. So, especially in small events, make it possible for the next horse to enter the arena and make his way to the start while the previous horse is finishing his round. The finish should be reasonably close to the exit but competitors should not be allowed to canter straight out of the arena. This is not only dangerous but very bad training for the horse who must be taught to turn away from the gate and then trot quietly out on a long rein.

Outdoors, the nearest part of an obstacle jumped away from the end of the arena should be at least 18 m (60 ft) from the end. The nearest part of an obstacle jumped towards the end of the arena should be at least 15 m (50 ft) from the end.

Always try to find time to analyse what happened over the course after the event. To do this you will need a copy of the judges' score sheet from which to find the following information:

- How many clear rounds? (How many did you expect?)
- How many eliminations and retirements? (Is this acceptable?)
- How many times was each fence faulted? Was any fence faulted too often? Why? Which fences caused no faults? Why?
- What was the average number of faults per round jumped?
- Did the course work to a climax, or were the last few fences jumped without faults right through the class?

When you are building a course yourself, or when you are watching competitions over someone else's tracks, it is important to know exactly what happens and work out the reasons for success or failure.

In this way you can gradually build up a library of ideas for design, and if you are wise your library will include both what is good and what should be avoided. Eventually, this library will be in your mind, experience filed away in the storage bins of your brain, from which the computer – memory – can accept or reject ideas as they occur during the planning process.

Planning on paper is only a part of the job and, however much trouble has been taken at this stage, the good course designer will always ride his own course in his mind and make alterations while actually building the fences, if he sees an improvement that ought to be made.

Often a course designer is congratulated on the cleverness of a test he never intended (which he no doubt accepts with becoming modesty!). Equally, often one sees unintentional horrors appearing on the course, which one can only hope the competitors can cope with and thereby save us from our own mistakes. Tolerances in height, width and distance, especially over big tracks, become very small, and minute variations can spell out the difference between classic success and awful disaster.

7 ◇ *Water*

The water jump is a bogey to many riders, primarily because so many arenas do not have one. This is unfortunate because it is part of the stock-in-trade of a show jumper to meet every kind of fence with the same confidence. If it is possible to build a water jump, or a fence over water, into an arena it should be done.

In order to give the course designer more flexibility the water jump should be constructed so that it can be jumped in both directions. The water should not be too shallow as this encourages horses to splash through it, nor so deep as to be dangerous if a horse fails to clear it. A depth of 0.3 m (12 ins) to 0.35 m (14 ins) in the middle is about right.

It is almost impossible to construct such a fence that will suit both top grade and novice horses. The object of putting a water jump in a novice class is to encourage them to jump it easily and willingly, whereas in a major competition it is there to test the horse's ability. Thus, for inexperienced horses the water jump should ideally vary between 2.4 m (8 ft) and 3.6 m (12 ft), while in the case of horses that are ready for more testing competitions it should vary between 3.6 m (12 ft) and 5 m (16 ft). Even constructing it so as to be able to achieve a 1.4 m (4 ft) variation presents considerable problems.

There are two ways of presenting a water jump. One is with a low slanting hedge (or brush box) in front of the water, the other is simply with a sloping plank or a white pole pegged to the ground. Using a brush box does give some flexibility, depending on where it is placed in relation to the front edge of the water itself. Fig. 27 shows a 3 m (10 ft) wide water jump, with an 0.5 m (1 ft 6 in) high brush fence set so as to make a measured width of anything between 2.4 m (8 ft) and 3.6 m (12 ft). This is done by having a series of 30 cm (1 ft) wide planks which can be placed over the water by means of strong blocks shaped to fit the profile of the excavation. By resting the brush fence on top of the planks the width to be jumped is reduced, and by placing it in front of the water (and removing the planks) the width is increased. An added asset of this system is that the whole water jump can be boarded over when not in use.

However, in whatever manner the fence is constructed it must be broader than the width that the horse has to jump. This breadth should be a minimum of 5 m (16 ft). One of the most beautiful water jumps in the world is the one at Hickstead. The breadth of this is ample and the jumping width is 4.3 m (14 ft 6 ins). In this magnificent arena there is plenty of room for water-filled ditches and obstacles with water of much variety. See photos 31 and 32.

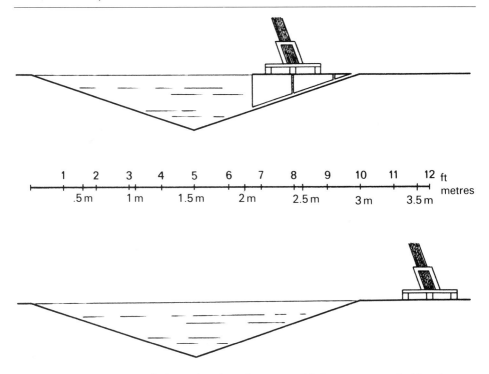

Fig. 27 *A water jump which can be adjusted to any width between 2.4 m (8 ft) and 3.6 m (12 ft).*

A water jump may have both a pole over the water and a white lath to mark the landing edge. In major classes it is unusual to place a pole over the water, as this makes it easier to jump. For this reason a pole is often used in minor classes to encourage less-experienced horses to jump water with confidence.

The edge of the water must be marked with a wooden lath or tape 5 m (2 ins) wide or some other clearly defined material. At many big shows strips of plasticine are used – they are ideal because the imprint of a horse's foot is clearly marked for the judge to see if he is in any doubt as to whether the jump was cleared or not.

The one vital factor in water jump construction is that all the levels must be exact. If they are right the water will reach the lip of the excavation simultaneously on both sides (take-off and landing) and will be constant all the way along both edges. It is extremely difficult to build on anything except absolutely level ground and is a job for a craftsman. Nothing is more infuriating than to find that the water reaches the lath on one side with 5 cm (2 ins) still to be filled on the other. Once it is wrong there is nothing that can be done about it except to start again.

A thick shock-absorbent mat of rubber or coconut matting must be placed on the landing side of the fence. If possible it should be one single strip of material that will lie flat both on the concrete and on the turf on the landing side, so that the water fills absolutely straight along the line of the lath. The mat must extend well

Photo 31   *The beautiful water jump at Hickstead. In the Derby this is 4.50 m (15 ft) wide.*

Photo 32   *The famous double of water ditches at Hickstead. As shown, this is a double of Liverpools. The distance between the two sets of rails is 7.25 m (23 ft 9 ins). A very difficult double if your horse does not like water.*

beyond the edge of the concrete so that there is no danger of it slipping and of the horse jarring its foot on bare concrete.

If you build a water jump in a permanent arena that is often used (and such an arena should have a water jump) you will find that if you do not take action the ground will deteriorate on both sides. The best thing to do is to dig out the turf to a depth of about 30 cm (1 ft). Then put in a base of stone which is tightly rolled and on top of which you put a permeable membrane. You can then top up with any suitable material such as you would use for construction of a sand arena. This should be done for at least two strides (7.50 m/24 ft) before and after the fence. If your water jump judge or an arena steward is equipped with a rake you can keep this fence in perfect condition for years. The advantages are enormous, as those whose horses learned to jump water in the 'Club' ring at Arena North in the 1970s will testify. The water can be included in just about every competition – riders can be allowed to practice over it to their heart's content without any deterioration of the ground.

I think that most course builders will agree that they have had more problems with water jump construction than any other fence. It is very difficult to build temporary ones that work out properly. Advice on construction is well worth seeking and the work itself needs to be done by an expert.

If it is not possible to construct a water jump in a particular arena, it may be in order to make a dry ditch. There are many attractive variations in fences that can be used over a ditch and it goes a part of the way towards teaching horses to jump water. Once they are accustomed to jumping over 'holes in the ground' the worst of the problem is over. The edge of the ditch must be well defined and this can easily be done by pegging a pole strongly to the ground just in front of the lip.

A fence that I very much like to use is a 'Liverpool'. This is a ditch in front of a fence and can be built in very many ways – some easy to jump, some very difficult. The simple version has no ditch at all and is simply a take-off rail placed in front of a normal vertical fence. It actually helps a horse to take off at the right spot so that his normal jump for a vertical will easily clear the fence (see Fig. 28).

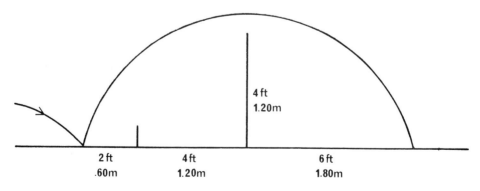

Fig. 28 *A simple version of the Liverpool fence.*

Photo 33   *The Liverpool fence. A notional ditch in front of rails.*

Photo 34   *A similar fence but with a wide water-filled ditch in front of nine slim poles. Stockholm Olympics, 1956.*

A similar fence, but much more difficult, is shown in Photo 34. It was first used at the CSI in Wiesbaden in 1956, the year of the Stockholm Olympic Games. Some, rightly as it transpired, guessed that the fence would be used at Stockholm and I know that both the Germans and the British were prepared for it.

Nevertheless, it caused a mass of faults at the Games. The photograph, reproduced from the German book of the Olympics, *Kavalkade* by Hans Köhler, shows Fritz Thiedemann on the immortal Meteor at this fence. There was a 2.10 m (7 ft) wide water-filled ditch in front of nine slim, blue and white poles 1.50 m (5 ft) high. Incidentally, there were only two clear rounds altogether over the two rounds of this difficult but beautiful course. They were both in the second round and were by Hans Winkler – riding Halle with ruptured stomach muscles – (gold) and Raimondo d'Inzo – Merano (silver). West Germany and Italy took gold and silver team honours and Britain won the bronze. The British team was Wilf White – Nizefela, Pat Smythe – Flanagan and Peter Robson – Scorchin.

WATER RELATED TO OTHER FENCES

To place fences at related distances, before or after water, is to set a very severe test and should be avoided unless you are sure that you know what you are doing.

Before a water jump
Let us first examine a fence placed before a water jump. The horse will be asked to lengthen his stride going into the water, so it is fair to assume that the distance between the fence and the water should be longer. On the other hand the take-off point at a water jump must be as close as possible to the fence, so this will make the distance shorter again. Practical experience has shown me that a distance of 26.5 m (87 ft) will be just right – that is, 90 cm (3 ft) longer than the general rule.

The distance results from an increase in the length of stride coupled with the need to take off close to the fence, and will involve six non-jumping strides, an average of 3.95 m (13 ft) long. Fig. 29 shows this in more detail. This is not to say, of course, that every horse will conform to this pattern. In a case like this where there is plenty of room, some riders collect after the first fence and go for seven strides so as to be sure of taking off right up against the water. One or two, doubtful of their horse's courage or willingness to stretch, might try for five strides but this would be more likely to produce faults than not. An analysis of the striding is made in Fig. 29 which shows that the distance could be shortened by 4 m (13 ft), total 22.6 m (74 ft), for one less stride, or to 18.8 m (61 ft) for two less.

After a water jump
Placing a fence at a related distance after a water jump creates a much more severe test than the one we have just considered and one that requires much more skill to ride. It is more difficult to say what will be the normal striding into a fence after water because horses of different temperament will react differently. The perfectly trained horse, having given a grand extension over the water, say 5.2 m (17 ft), over a 4.2 m (14 ft) water jump, will land with a lot of forward movement which must be lost within the next three strides and then recreated on a powerful controlled stride to the fence. This will be especially difficult if the fence is a vertical and less so if it is any kind of staircase obstacle.

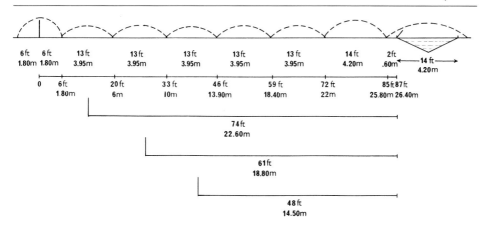

Fig. 29 *A fence placed before a water jump. This figure shows:*
26.40 m (87 ft) between fences for six non-jumping strides.
22.60 m (74 ft) between fences for five non-jumping strides.
18.80 m (61 ft) between fences for four non-jumping strides.
14.50 m (48 ft) between fences for three non-jumping strides.

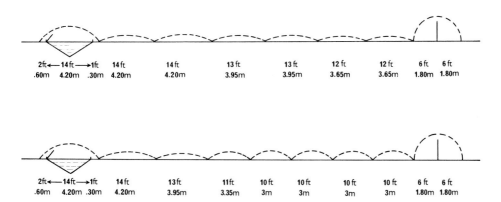

Fig. 30 *Two possible stride diagrams for either six or seven strides between a water jump and an upright fence 25.80 m (85 ft) apart.*

The distances shown in Figs. 29 and 30 are based on the obstacle that is related to the water jump being a vertical fence. If it is not a vertical, but a parallel or staircase type of fence, the distance would have to be shortened, as explained in detail in Chapter 6. Fig. 30 shows a smooth loss of length of stride in such a test. Many horses would be less likely to succeed in going for six strides rather than the seven-stride pattern, which enables horse and rider to achieve a greater degree of collection out of which to jump the vertical fence. The closer any fence is placed to the water, the more difficult it will very rapidly become.

An analysis of a combination of these problems is shown in Fig. 31. Because of

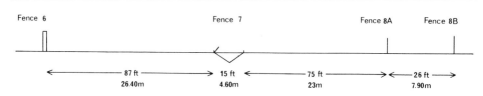

Fig. 31   *Fence 6. Wall 1.50 m (5 ft).*
Fence 7. Water 4.60 m (15 ft).
Fence 8A. Vertical planks and poles 1.40 m (4 ft 6 ins).
Fence 8B. Vertical planks and poles 1.45 m (4 ft 9 ins).

the double of vertical fences, competitors could not afford to go too strongly into the 4.60 m (15 ft) water jump. They had to have a horse that would stretch over the water confidently and calmly. On landing they had to lose forward momentum very rapidly while retaining impulsion and gathering collection so as to arrive at the take-off point for the double in the right state. Out of twenty horses that qualified for this championship, eight were clear over this difficult test. The competition was won in a five-horse jump-off.

This particular test was set in the White Horse Whisky Championship, held at the Rand Show (CSI) in Johannesburg in 1977 and was beautifully jumped. The whole of this course is shown in Fig. 15.

I think it would be a very rare occasion that would see a water jump used in a combination, although fences with water are often used in doubles. (Photo 32.)

If you are not too confident about setting fences before or after water, you can offset them at an angle to the water to give the rider more chance to adjust the stride.

8 ◇ *Indoor Jumping*

For atmosphere, excitement and a sense of close involvement among spectators, indoor jumping cannot be beaten. This is why the great indoor shows almost invariably play to full houses, like the best theatrical productions. The course designer fills the role of stage manager even more obviously than outdoors. He must be even more conscious of the need to entertain spectators for he is, in part, also the script writer.

Indoors, as out, there are two kinds of show – spectator shows and rider shows. The same criteria apply for these as for those that have already been discussed.

The most important single factor in preparing an indoor course is the going and there are many different mixtures that can be used. A clay subsoil – about 0.15 m (6 ins) thick if laid on a hard floor – must be rolled level and firm before adding the jumping surface. Wattle bark, after it has been processed for tanning leather, makes an excellent springy, durable surface. A mixture of sand and shavings in a proportion of 1 to 3 is often used and I have also seen chopped plastic granules and chopped rubber from old tyres used, both of which produced good, springy surfaces that were free of dust.

Whatever surface is used a regular dressing of coarse salt is essential. This maintains the structure of the material by attracting moisture and preventing it from breaking up into dust. The brighter the surface the more attractive, and the less expensive, the lighting – which is all-important. Dull lighting, even if sufficient for the actual jumping, does spoil the atmosphere where brilliance is a vital ingredient.

Anyone proposing to lay an indoor surface should consult an expert before becoming involved in the very considerable expense.

Outdoors, poles should be 4.2 m (14 ft) long. Indoors 3.6 m (12 ft) is an acceptable length. I hate heavy poles and believe the ideal to be 9 cms (3½ ins) diameter – preferably planed so that they are the same either end. Colours must be carefully thought out to avoid the danger of fences merging with their background.

Length of stride indoors is not appreciably shorter than outside, providing that the going is right. If you are faced with heavy going you must shorten the distances. I have found that the multiples of 3.6 m (12 ft) between fences works very well indoors and encourages bold, onward-bound jumping. However, in doubles and trebles that end up close to a crowded arena wall, horses are likely to hedge off a bit and a long distance out of the combination might prove difficult.

The distance from the ends of the arena to a fence is a key factor in indoor course building: Fig. 32 shows that, if you place a fence to be jumped away from the end of an arena at the 18.5 m (60 ft) mark, the normal competitor will have three strides on a straight approach to the fence. This will not prove difficult, whereas a novice horse would find 14.5 m (48 ft) a more severe test. I do not like putting a fence closer to the end than about 14.5 m (48 ft).

On the other side of the arena a parallel fence is shown, jumped towards the end, on the 14.5 m (48 ft) mark. This leaves two strides in a straight line although, if the rider is not concentrating, his horse will drift off to the left and make the approach to the next fence more difficult. Once again I would not like to place a fence closer to the end of the arena than this.

Simplicity has already been stressed as a guide to good course design outdoors. In the confined indoor arena it is even more valid. The golden rule of building indoors is *don't put too many fences in the arena*. Those who are setting tracks indoors for the first time cannot go wrong if they produce a straightforward line in an uncluttered arena.

Space is the special problem that confronts the course builder and halls that are

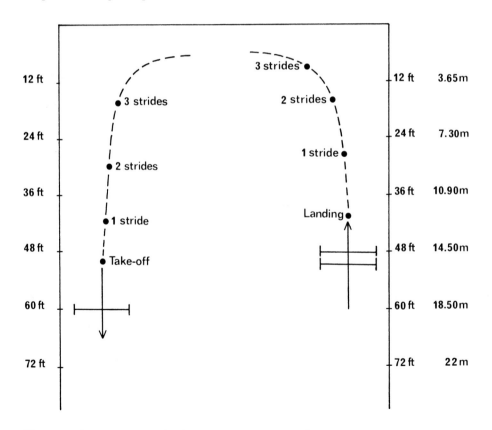

Fig. 32 *Coming out of and riding into corners of an indoor arena.*

less than about 60 m (200 ft) long by 30 m (100 ft) wide are not ideal. I would rather have the full width than the full length if one had to be sacrificed. A narrow hall greatly restricts the freedom of action of the course builder.

To save time it is a good idea to mark the distances on the two long-side walls – or better still to nail a tape measure along the whole length of the wall. Most indoor halls are built in bays, so if you know the width of each bay you will have a good idea of how the distances will work out. Alan Ball, who is probably the most experienced indoor builder in the world, uses what he calls his 'cabbage lines' (they are just string wound round a spool) to set his fences on the diagonals in a straight line. Always decide which fence on a diagonal you must build first, set it in place and take your 'cabbage line' from there.

It is absolutely essential to design your courses exactly to scale when working indoors. Graph paper makes this easy, probably using a square on the paper to represent 10 m. You need to know the exact width of the fences, including wings, so that you can plot the uncluttered lines that will produce fluent and attractive jumping.

The three course plans that follow (see Figs. 33, 34 and 35) were used at a BSJA affiliated show and provided some excellent jumping. There is nothing unusual about them but they fulfil the criteria of simplicity and space. I built them at the invitation of Bruce Ross in his superb 60 m (200 ft) by 30 m (100 ft) indoor hall at the Parkgate Centre at Osbaldeston in Lancashire – a winter Mecca for show jumpers in the north of England. Note the comments written against the fences relating to changes for the next competition. By planning all alterations before the show, course-changing times were negligible and yet there was plenty of variety between the three tracks.

A detail sheet was made out for each of the course plans built at the Parkgate Centre. I have included one here used in conjunction with the Class 1 competition (see Fig. 33).

For Class 2 (see Fig. 34) I have not used another detail sheet but simply marked how the changes are to be made on the course builder's own plan. 'Stet' means that the fence stays in the same position as before. Only new distances between fences are marked on this plan. The words 'ex fence 4' means use material from fence 4 in the previous class.

For Class 3 (see Fig. 35) the important issue was the exact siting of fences 4, 8 and 9. Fence 9C was to be 15 m (50 ft) from the end of the arena and was the first of these fences to be built. Then the rest of the combination was set and finally the angling of fences 4 and 8 so as to ensure a good approach from fence 7 to fence 8.

However carefully courses are drawn to scale, the art of course building lies in building on the ground itself. A slavish following of a paper plan will never produce a result as good as that achieved when careful planning is combined with a horseman's appreciation of the problems.

Great care must be taken when measuring courses indoors. Experience proves that indoors the track must be generously measured to avoid having too many horses incurring time penalties.

By way of contrast, Fig. 36 shows a course that I built at an international show

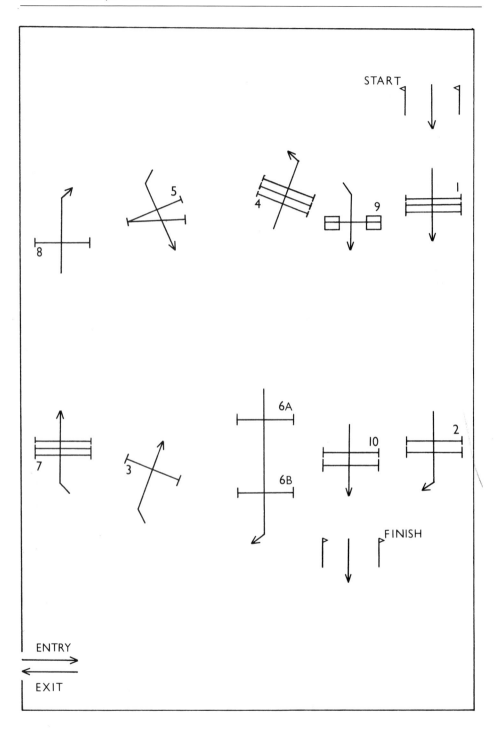

Fence	Description	Height	Spread	Distance	Remarks
1	Straw bales and poles	1 m (3 ft 3 ins)	1 m (3 ft 3 ins)	15.10 m (50 ft) from wall	
2	Parallel with low wall base	1.10 m (3 ft 6 ins)	1.10 m (3 ft 6 ins)	22 m (72 ft)	
3	Horizontal poles with crossed poles	1 m (3 ft 3 ins)	—	21.40 m (70 ft) from wall	
4	Triple bar	0.85 m/1 m/1.10 m (2 ft 9 ins/3 ft 3 ins/ 3 ft 6 ins)	1.40 m (4 ft 6 ins)	22.50 m (84 ft)	
5	V fence	adjust when setting	—	—	Site to give best approach to 6A
6A	Upright poles over pickets	1.10 m (3 ft 6 ins)	—	22 m (72 ft)	
6B	Upright poles	1.10 m (3 ft 6 ins)	—	7.50 m (24 ft 6 ins)	
7	Wall with pole behind	1 m/1.10 m (3 ft 3 ins/3 ft 6 ins)	1.10 m (3 ft 6 ins)	—	
8	Upright poles over rustic filler	1.10 m (3 ft 6 ins)	—	18.50 m (60 ft)	
9	Narrow upright stile between wall sections	1.10 m (3 ft 6 ins)	—	—	
10	Parallel over hurdles	1.10 m/1.10 m (3 ft 6 ins/3 ft 6 ins)	1.10 m (3 ft 6 ins)	22 m (72 ft)	

Fig. 33 *Parkgate – Lancashire. Class 1. Newcomers' competition. Table: A2. Speed: 320 m/ min. (350 yds/min.). Distance: 385 m (421 yds). Jump-off fences: 1, 4, 5, 6, 7, 10. Distance: 320 m (350 yds). Arena: 60 × 30 m (200 × 100 ft).*

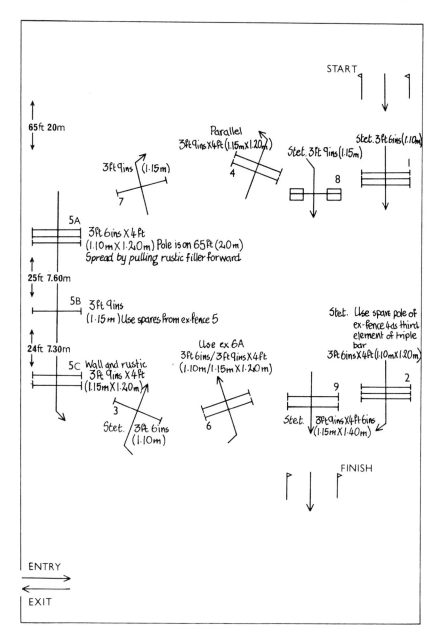

Fig. 34 *Parkgate-Lancashire. Class 2. Foxhunter Competition. Table: A3. Speed: 320 m/ min. (350 yds/min.). Distance: 372 m (408 yds). Jump-off fences: 1, 4, 5, 6, 7, 8, 9. Distance: 320 m. The notes on this course plan were written so that I could make a very quick change at the end of Class 1. This was done and in a few moments we produced a very different course for this class.*

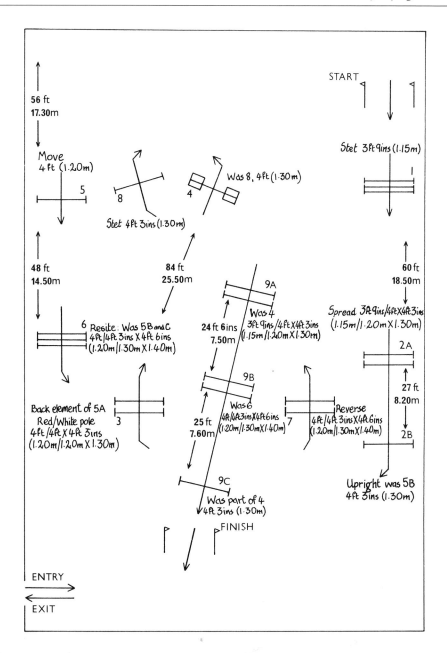

Fig. 35 *Parkgate-Lancashire. Class 3. Open Jumping. Table: A3. Speed: 350 m/min. (382 yds/min.). Distance: 385 m (420 yds). Jump-off fences: 1, 2, 3, 6, 8, 9. Distance: 320 m (350 yds).*

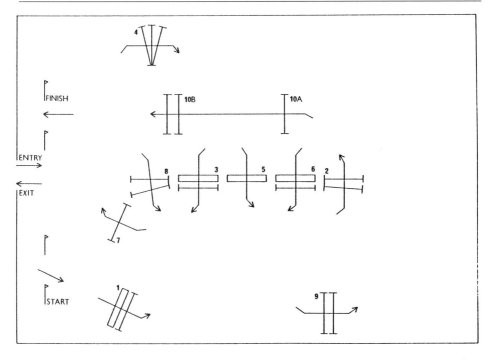

Fig. 36 *Bulawayo Indoor Show – CSI, 1968. The Dunlop Speed Competition. Table: C. Speed: 350 m/min. (382 yds/min.). Jump-off fences: 1, 2, 3, 4, 5, 9, 10.*

held in Rhodesia (now Zimbabwe) in 1968 and whose arena was 55 m (180 ft) by 30 m (100 ft). This was a speed class course for medium horses and produced a very exciting competition as well as an arena that looked unusual. Fences 3 and 6 and fences 2 and 8 were mirror images of each other.

Fig. 37 (overleaf) is the working plan used by Alan Ball at Olympia in 1988. It looks as if riders had five options from the three fences (5-6-7) into the closed combinations in the middle of the ring. Note the instruction to leave 2 m free of obstructions on both long sides for turning from 5B to 6A and 6B to 7A.

Photo 36 *Olympia, 1990. The Volvo World Cup Qualifier, designed by Paul Weier of Switzerland (see Chapter 13). The fences were beautifully decorated with the Christmas theme and made a superb spectacle.*

LEFT: **Photo 35** *Course building in progress at Olympia in 1990. You can clearly see the four teams under their own course designer, each of whom is responsible for a corner. Alan Ball is striding along (right-hand side of arena). Low-loading trailers take complete fence kits to the exact position where they are required. The course takes ten to twenty minutes to put up from scratch under Alan Ball's marvellous management.*

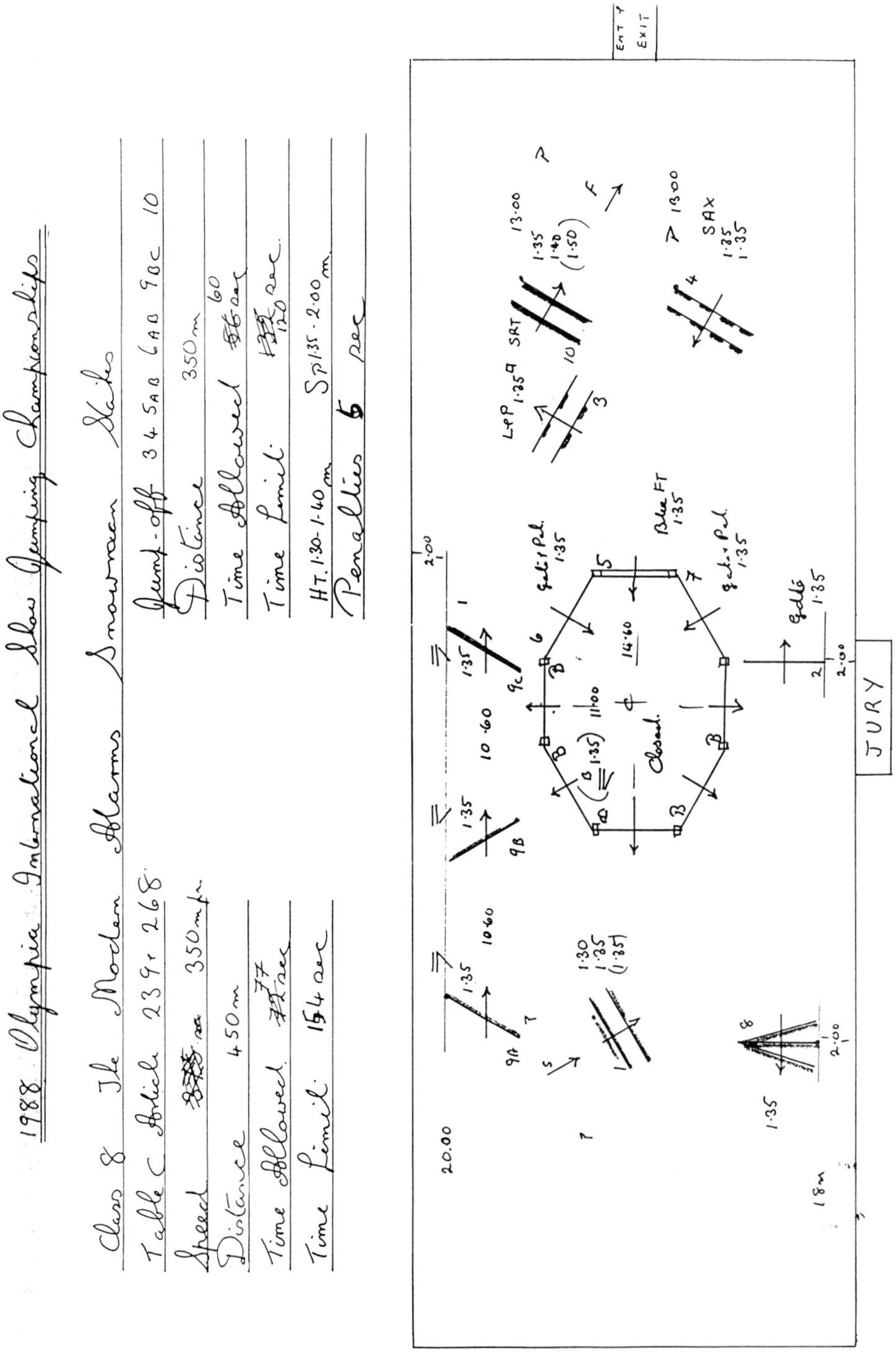

Fig. 37 *1988 Olympia International Show Jumping Championships.*

9 ◈ Courses for Ponies

I hope that what I have so far said about course designing bears out my commitment to achieving courses that are inviting and flowing, and which encourage horses and riders to ride a bold, onward-bound, rhythmical round.

No country in the world produces quality ponies as good, and in such numbers, as does Britain. These ponies can really use themselves to cover the ground with powerful, ground-devouring strides. This is an asset that course designers should exploit by encouraging ponies to jump with confidence and to use themselves over fences and not merely go up and down like a lift. Too many trainers of ponies (and some course designers) are obsessed by height. There is nothing particularly clever in jumping 1.4 m (4 ft 6 ins) uprights if at the same time you are worried by a decent size spread.

Ponies that are not particularly well made or well trained (or both) do canter on a very short stride, but both in their training and in their jumping they ought to be made to improve this defect. Course designers who pander to this weakness only make it worse where it is inherent and spoil the power and rhythm of better animals.

Having tested and measured many, many times the striding distance that ponies cover from take-off to landing and their stride after landing, I can state as a *fact* that once a pony is going on boldly at its fences, the distances per stride should only be shortened as follows:

Pony of 14.2 hh – 30 cm (1 ft) – Average length of stride at canter – 3.30 m (11 ft)

Pony of 13.2 hh – 60 cm (2 ft) – Average length of stride at canter – 3.00 m (10 ft)

Pony of 12.2 hh – 90 cm (3 ft) – Average length of stride at canter – 2.70 m (9 ft).

The likelihood that many ponies will find these distances long, is due to the way in which course designers and trainers exaggerate this shorter stride until they are almost obliged to scratch around the course. I once had a dog, a Dobermann/Ridgeback cross, who followed my horse over fences when I was schooling. Over doubles he took the same striding as the horse! So, if a 6 hh dog can do it, I am sure a 14 hh pony must be able to.

If we look again at Fig. 23, the table of easy distances for horses in combinations, and apply the reductions for ponies given above we can now give distances for the three height groups of ponies (see Fig. 38). These can be used as a rule-of-thumb guide, always remembering the other variable factors that must be taken into account. Training over low parallel and spread fences encourages the pony to jump correctly. Good training followed by experience over flowing, bold,

Over 13.2 and up to 14.2 hh				
		SECOND FENCE		
		Upright	Parallel	Staircase
FIRST FENCE	Upright	7.30 m (24 ft)	7 m (23 ft)	6.70 m (22 ft)
	Parallel	7.60 m (25 ft)	7.30 m (24 ft)	7 m (23 ft)
	Staircase	7.90 m (26 ft)	7.60 m (25 ft)	7.30 m (24 ft)
FOR TWO STRIDES ADD 3 m (10 ft)				

Over 12.2 and up to 13.2 hh				
		SECOND FENCE		
		Upright	Parallel	Staircase
FIRST FENCE	Upright	7 m (23 ft)	6.70 m (22 ft)	6.40 m (21 ft)
	Parallel	7.30 m (24 ft)	7 m (23 ft)	6.70 m (22 ft)
	Staircase	7.60 m (25 ft)	7.30 m (24 ft)	7 m (23 ft)
FOR TWO STRIDES ADD 2.70 m (9 ft)				

Over 12.2 hh				
		SECOND FENCE		
		Upright	Parallel	Staircase
FIRST FENCE	Upright	6.70 m (22 ft)	6.40 m (21 ft)	6 m (20 ft)
	Parallel	7 m (23 ft)	6.70 m (22 ft)	6.40 m (21 ft)
	Staircase	7.30 m (24 ft)	7 m (23 ft)	6.70 m (22 ft)
FOR TWO STRIDES ADD 2.40 m (8 ft)				

Fig. 38 *Table of easy distances in combinations, for ponies.*

encouraging courses will produce an even higher standard of junior jumping than that which we presently enjoy.

The simple principles that were listed in Chapter 4 apply to ponies just as much as, and in many cases even more than, to horses – in particular, problems concerned with the exit from the arena, since children probably do not have the strength to ride a pony strongly away from or past it. Of course there comes a point at which they have got to go away from the exit, but this must be made as easy as possible. The fence must not only be positioned with great care but also must be as simple as possible and the type of fence that they are very familiar with, such as upright poles, low brush and pole, straw bales and pole and so on.

Let us look at Fig. 38 in more detail. By customary British standards the distances given may be considered a little on the long side. I would start the show by putting these distances about 30 cm (1 ft) shorter and try to end the show with the ponies jumping these distances with ease and confidence. *Do not use spreads out of combinations for novices or ponies under 12.2 hh except in high-class and championship competitions.*

A test set for a junior competition at Arena North, is shown in Fig. 39. Wooden

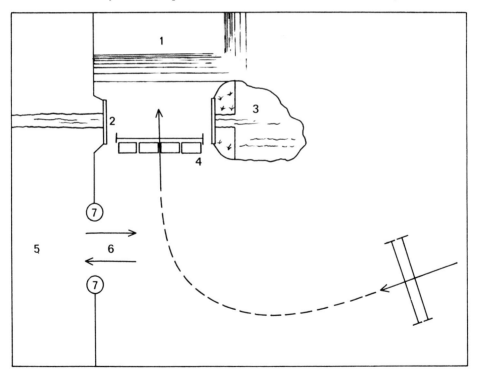

Fig. 39 *Key:* 1. *High bank*
             2. *Bridge over stream*
             3. *Pond*
             4. *Wooden beer barrels with red/white poles*

5. *Collecting ring*
6. *Entrance exit*
7. *Stone towers*

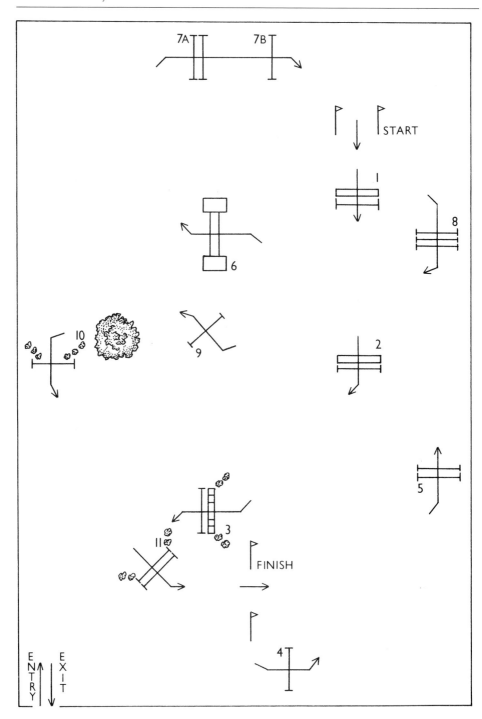

Fence	Description	Height	Spread	Distance	Remarks
1	Brush with white pole behind	0.90/1 m (3 ft/3 ft 3 ins)	1.15 m (3 ft 9 ins)	27.50 m (90 ft)	From end of arena
2	Low wall with red/white pole behind	1 m/1.10 m (3 ft 3 ins/3 ft 6 ins)	1.20 m (4 ft)	24.50 m (80 ft)	
3	Parallel of yellow/white poles over straw bales	1.10/1.10 m (3 ft 6 ins/3 ft 6 ins)	1.20 m (4 ft)	—	Shrubs on L/H side
4	Rustic pole over brush fence – vertical	1.10 m (3 ft 6 ins)	—	—	Site past centre of arena
5	Liverpool of blue/white poles with flower boxes	0.30/1.10 m (1 ft/3 ft 6 ins)	1.20 m (4 ft)	—	Flower boxes under front pole
6	Wall with pillars	1.15 m (3 ft 9 ins)	—	—	
7A	Spread fence green/white poles over hurdles with pole behind	0.90/1 m (3 ft/3 ft 3 ins)	1.10 m (3 ft 6 ins)	—	
7B	Vertical green/white poles	1.10 m (3 ft 6 ins)	—	7.30 m (24 ft)	
8	Triple bar yellow/white poles	0.85/1 m/1.15 m (2 ft 9 ins/3 ft 3 ins/ 3 ft 9 ins)	1.45 m (4 ft 9 ins)	—	Completely filled with birch branches
9	White gate	1.10 m (3 ft 6 ins)	—	—	
10	6 ft wide style of rustic poles	1.10 m (3 ft 6 ins)	—	—	Use full-width poles. Ponies to jump through gap in trees set into turf
11	White poles as parallel over log-type filler	1.10 m/1.15 m (3 ft 6 ins/3 ft 9 ins)	1.30 m (4 ft 3 ins)	—	Shrubs on R/H side

Fig. 40 *Class for ponies not exceeding 13.2 hh.*
Jump-off fences: 1, 2, 6, 7A, 7B, 8, 9, 10.

Notes: Fence 1   *Far from and towards exit.*

Fence 2   *Nice spread to encourage bold jumping.*

Fence 3   *Well shrubbed on left side to avoid running out towards exit.*

Fence 4   *Sited past the centre line so that those hesitating past exit can get going again.*

Fence 5   *Must ride boldly into this fence.*

Fence 6   *Pony must be kept full of impulsion here as he gets further from exit.*

Fence 7A–B   *Double at far end from exit. Spread to upright is easy and safe.*

Fence 8   *Big, strong fence in an easy position will produce good jumping.*

Fence 9   *Needs accurate riding. A good (safe) test after the triple bar.*

Fence 10   *Set to catch the rider who loses concentration towards the end of the course. Fence suits the terrain.*

Fence 11   *Big, powerful end to the competition to give riders a sense of achievement. Note position of the shrubs.*

beer barrels with a pole just behind them were placed as a jump on to the bridge, which was placed past the entrance and exit gate leading to the collecting ring. It was practically certain that a large number of ponies would refuse here – which indeed they did. This illustrates the principle that I mentioned earlier. When siting a fence after the exit gate for ponies (especially small ponies) *always* leave plenty of room for the pony to turn away and get going again before he is committed to the fence.

Do remember also that small ponies are much stronger than small children and will only jump if they are willing to do so. And keep in mind the fact that little ponies are very good at counting to three and once they have stopped are often difficult to start again. The course designer, therefore, has the duty of building courses which are so inviting that it will not enter the mind of a reasonable pony to refuse to jump. Once a pony has got into the habit of jumping freely he is a superb schoolmaster and will give children some wonderful sport. Course designers who are sensitive to these points can help very greatly in the production of marvellous little jumpers.

Fig. 40 shows a course designed for up to and including 13.2 hh ponies. Heights of fences are shown at around 1.10 m (3 ft 6 ins), but this could alter depending on the standard of entries in the competition. This course should prove very inviting and encourage bold riding, as well as giving the children something to think about and a sense of achievement at the finish. It is a very straightforward track with three changes of rein. All the approaches are fair and should cause no difficulty. There is a good distribution of vertical, parallel and staircase fences. The jump-off also has a good distribution of types of fence and two changes of rein. The location of the exit should cause no problems on this course. The course works to a climax with concentration needed at the last three fences, number 11 being slightly bigger than any other. When built on the ground it should provide a very good competition. Every fence has a purpose.

This analysis of what is, essentially, a very everyday course shows how much time and thought is necessary if the course designer is to provide successful competitions at any level. Having planned the course, just as much trouble must also be taken in setting it up on the ground. In this case the siting of fences 9 and 11, in particular, must be just right to ensure a good line of approach.

Experienced horses and ponies can get a course designer out of all sorts of trouble, but in this sort of class you cannot afford to make mistakes. Senior course designers are performing a valuable service if they can sometimes manage to spare some time for novice horses and ponies.

10 ◇ *Courses for Horse Trials*

W e are extremely lucky in Britain to have the most wonderful cross-country courses. You never get a bad course and the reason is that cross-country course designing and building takes months of work and thought. 'Genius means transcendent capacity of taking trouble' (Carlyle). Our national genius for cross-country riding stems largely from the genius as defined by Carlyle of our course designers and builders. They are dedicated people who take a vast pride in what they are doing, are ultra-sensitive to how their course rides and to comments by riders and spectators. The result is that the courses are not only technically excellent but they also look marvellous – the presentation of the fences plays a major part in the thinking of those responsible for it.

Alas! The same cannot be said for the show jumping at horse trials, where often a set of damaged, scarred and ugly fences are hurriedly assembled into a boring figure-of-eight pattern by a course designer who is too busy or too uninterested to take the time to think about what he might be able to do to make his contribution, small as it is, match up with the efforts of the cross-country builder and the event organiser. Presumably the model must be Badminton or Burghley. Jon Doney's courses at Badminton with their truly beautiful and unique fences (more original and attractive even than the best horse show fences anywhere in Britain) are the ultimate (see Photos 45–51). Course plans for the show jumping at Badminton in 1989 and 1990 are shown with comments by Jon. Photos 41–44 show the lovely fences at Burghley in 1990 built by Nick Staines, and are contrasted with the really appalling presentation of the show jumps at a one-day horse trial in Suffolk.

Although, in terms of penalties, the show jumping is relatively unimportant, it is often right at the heart of the event with the secretary, score board, trade stands and catering around it. It should make an excellent centrepiece to the whole and be a compliment, not an insult, to the organisers, competitors and public. Of course there are many excellent one-day event show jumping arenas and courses – Milton Keynes, Gatcombe and Tidworth are just three that come to mind. Here real thought has gone into the siting of the arena and the layout of the event, with spectators very much in mind as well as the actual show jumping course and its presentation.

I find it incomprehensible that any course designer worth his salt can fail to produce a beautiful course. Surely it is a dream opportunity to be able to build a course in your own time, without the usual rush to put it up and clear it away

Photos 37–38 *A little trouble taken in preparing fences can make all the difference in their final appearance. The untidy fence above is made attractive by the addition of simple course-building material* (below).

again between displays or with half a dozen other different competitions to cater for on the same day. It is a real set-piece affair. You can spend as long as you like building and decorating, knowing that you don't need to move a fence until the event is finished. A glorious opportunity.

All the rules and ideas in this book apply to courses at horse trials as much as anywhere else. But do not forget that the training of an event horse is different from that of a show jumper. Since an ability to gallop is amongst the most vital characteristics of a successful eventer, these horses are naturally more onward bound and a little longer striding. Distances, in combinations especially, should not be too short – as they very often are. It is much fairer and will encourage better jumping if the standard distances are used, and varied when a test is set, by longer rather than shorter distances. This will reward the on-going, easy-striding horse, which is the best type for eventing. At novice level it is important to give horses

Photos 39–40 *A sorry contrast to the lovely fences which follow are these at a one-day event. Here no effort whatever has been made to improve the appearance of this extremely tatty set of BSJA fences. Above: Why, for example, did no one think to put some green branches into this brush fence? Below: Repairs have been made to both wings, and the wood used has not even been painted. Note that the cross-country course at this event was beautifully built and presented.*

Photos 41–44 *Nothing is too much trouble when it comes to presenting magnificent fences at the big three-day events. These four fences, built by Nick Staines at Burghley in 1990, show what imagination and care can do.*

and riders every encouragement and the theory of inviting them into a line of fences or a combination with fences that start them off boldly applies more than ever. This is not to say that you must *never* use a short distance, just that it should be the exception and not the rule.

I think that in virtually every case the fences at BHS horse trials should be set at the maximum permitted height and spread. That is the official standard set for that event and it is a standard that all horses concerned should meet. Similarly, unlike pure show jumping where courses should not normally be very long, the course should be close to the maximum permitted length and number of obstacles. Eventers are not as a whole very good at the show jumping phase and you are unlikely to have to worry about getting enough penalties if you follow this advice. But do make your vertical fences true verticals and your parallels parallel, and do not always put in an overstrong groundline.

I once stood with a course builder who had built at a horse trial for the first time and he couldn't get over how bad the show jumping was. I did not remind him that the definition of a bad course is one that produces bad jumping. But nevertheless the general standard is not too good for the same reason that the dressage is less good on the whole than you would find at a purely dressage show. The training, preparation and level of fitness of an eventer are completely different from those of the show jumping specialist. Added to this is the riders' tension, brought on by the importance of achieving a clear round, which makes them less relaxed than they would be in a straight show jumping competition. This is because, in a season,

Photos 45–51   *Examples of Jon Doney's unique fences at Badminton 1991.* Below: *Fence 3, the Shire Horse Inn. The inn sign has a portrait of 'Master', the late Duke of Beaufort.*

Photos 46–47 *Fence 8, Badminton, 1991 – a beautiful double of the gates and church at Badminton. Below: Detail of Fence 8B.*

Photos 48–51   *Further examples of Jon Doney's perfectly designed and presented fences at the 1991 Badminton Horse Trials.*

a novice eventer will be lucky to compete in a total of about fifteen to twenty competitions, whereas a show jumper can do almost that number every month. A bad round will put paid to the hopes of a competitor for the whole event, so a great deal depends on the minute or so that he is in the show jumping arena.

Put in a minimum of two changes of direction in every course because suppleness and balance are key factors in the make up of an eventer. Make sure that your line encourages fluent jumping and brings out the best in the horses.

I also think that it is very important to measure the course correctly. Especially at novice level, if competitors get the idea that they will not incur time penalties no matter how slowly they go or how long a track they take, they will not learn to ride at the speed required by the rules. This is doing them no favours if and when they get higher up the scale.

Ideally if I was buying a horse to go eventing I would buy a good young show jumper that looked as if it could gallop. They have been taught to jump correctly, and if you can be more or less sure of a clear round in the show jumping it takes a lot of the worry out of the day. Provided they are bold, it also makes them safer and more sensible when it comes to awkward combinations across country.

If your eventer is not a good show jumper, and especially if it is an ex-racehorse, you must do lots of grid work and gymnastic exercises, including bounces and short strides into spread fences, to sharpen him up, get him basculing and snapping up his legs. Some details of this type of work are given in *Appendix C*.

If you are building for a three-day event do not forget that the horses have made a terrific effort the previous day. Here are Jon Doney's courses for Badminton together with his comments, from which I must highlight the line that sums up the philosophy of a man at the very top of his profession: '*I was pleased to watch horses enjoying themselves and jumping with confidence.*'

That indeed is what it is all about.

John Doney writes:

> 'The thought, when designing, was a general free-flowing course but with turns and angled fences to see if the horse was still concentrating and reacting to the rider's commands. The questions asked are not demanding but need concentration over a long course, especially when some fences are unusual and well decorated.
>
> 'It is important to make the course not only interesting to the horse and rider, but also interesting and pleasing to the public. (What a pity we don't let the public walk the courses for major events beforehand. Hickstead allowed this again this year – a great interest to them.)
>
> 'Whilst I realise that the show jumping phase is an important part of the whole event, I was pleased to watch horses enjoying themselves and jumping with confidence after the more difficult previous day.
>
> 'I believe that the show jumping phase should have a bearing on the result, as this year, without major problems that one might insert into show jumping courses.'

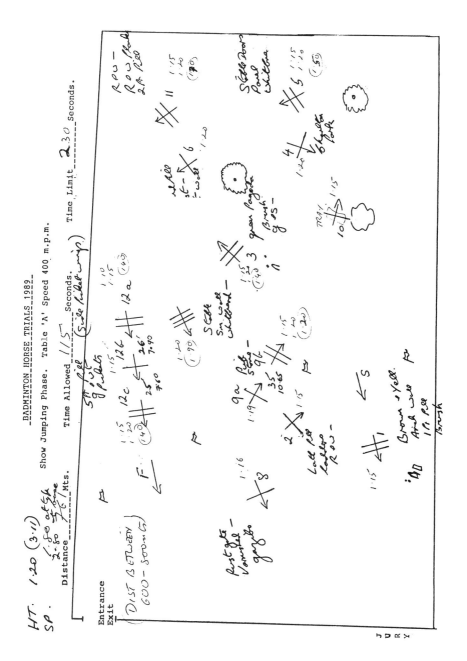

Fig. 41 *Jon Doney's course plan for Badminton, 1989.*

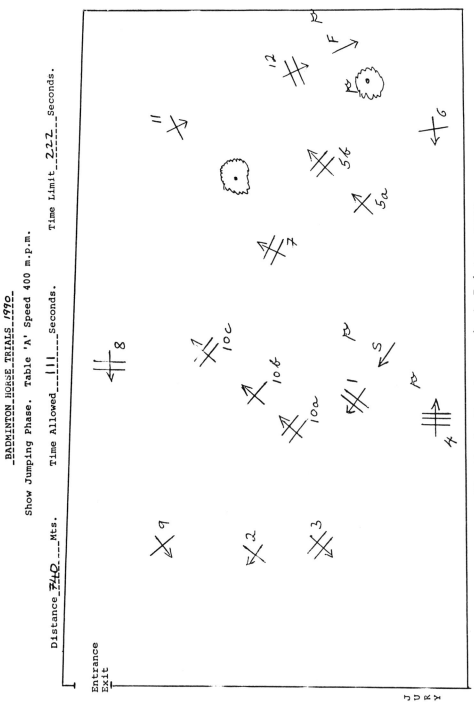

Fig. 42 *Jon Doney's course plan for Badminton, 1990.*

11 ◈ *Working Hunter Courses for Horses and Ponies*

The first criterion for working hunter and working hunter pony classes is that any decent hunter should get round the course. I well remember taking an Australian friend to Peterborough and waxing lyrical about our marvellous working hunter ponies. We arrived in time for the 14 hh class to witness the elimination of more than half the ponies. It was a complete disaster, not least because the course started directly away from the entrance. The simple principles outlined in Chapter 4 apply especially to working hunters, who will probably not have as much ring experience as the show jumpers.

The only guidelines given in the rules are that 'fences should have a natural appearance and not be easily dislodged'. The latter point is pretty clear – no flimsy fences and no light poles. When I build working hunter courses I think of a day's hunting and try to reproduce the sort of obstacles one might meet, especially in that locality.

The jumping part of working hunter judging is valued at 60% of the total marks obtainable. Of this, 40% is on faults (knock downs, refusals and falls) and 20% for style. So the course must, on the whole, be free-flowing so that the judge can see the horse flow on and meet inviting fences in its stride. At the same time I like to see one or more 'trappy' obstacles, such as a yard that has to be jumped into, followed by a turn before a jump out. It must, in fact, be a microcosm of a day's hunting and give the judge a chance to see plenty of difference in style so that he can use that 20% of the marks effectively.

Figure 43 shows a working hunter course at Arena North which was unusual and enjoyable. We also made the whole class follow the Holcombe hounds in a gallop around the lovely arena, over half a dozen small brush fences as a part of the final judging. It wasn't marked but any horse that blew up was put down the line. The point is that it was great fun *and* it attracted a crowd. As in the case of the horse trials, this is a great opportunity for a course designer to show his or her imagination and, by taking trouble, make a very good event out of it. There is usually plenty of time to make a really attractive picture.

Many organisations have special sets of working hunter/pony jumping equipment. It must be 'rustic' type material and strongly made. If you are short of material it is amazing how much you can do with brush frames (not filled like the awful one in photo 39 in the previous chapter), straw bales and trees – *plus* plenty of imagination. If you are able to go out and cut some natural timber with bark it is a lovely addition. I love to use unlevel poles with bumps and kinks, as these make

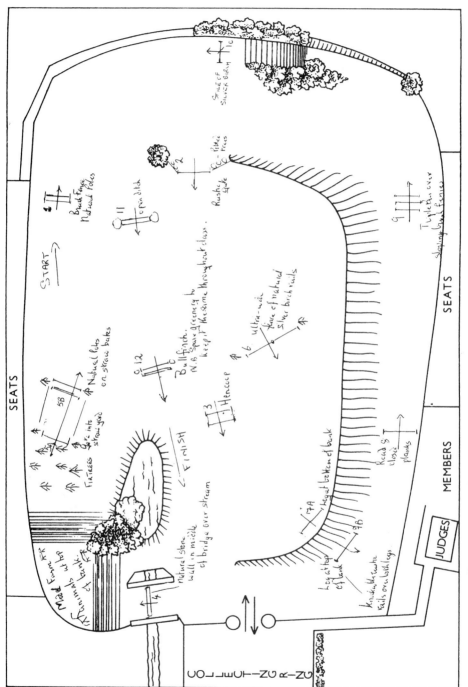

Fig. 43 *Lancashire International Horse Show – CSI. Arena North – 1st August 1975.*

the course look much more natural. There is, of course, no reason why you can't use walls painted as stone or brick as this is just the sort of obstacle you would meet hunting. It is also a good idea sometimes to offer alternatives. I remember Allan Oliver giving a super choice at the Devon County Show of a cattle grid (consisting of 5 cm (2 in.) diameter poles held in a pair of indented sleepers) or a gate at the maximum height. To add to the natural appearance it is nice to use double-width fences, which help to give the appearance of the real thing.

So, just a few reminders:

- Do not start your course away from the gate.
- Encourage bold, rhythmical jumping over a free-flowing track, but include one test at the sort of 'trappy' place you might find out hunting – but no 'tricks', just a test of handiness.
- Have as much variety and interest as you can think up.
- Make sure there is ample room to get at every fence.
- Have a couple of changes of direction.
- No flimsy fences.

Check the list of material on pages 38–39 in Chapter 3, all of which would help you

Photo 52 *A typical working hunter fence but with the wrong wings and looking much better from the front than from the back.*

build an interesting and original working hunter course.

It is a good idea to include a double in your course – probably to simulate a road crossing or jumping into and out of a yard. If you do, and if your double is placed where you expect the horse to be flowing on, do not make it a short distance. If you want to vary the standard distance, make it a little longer rather than a little shorter. A bounce, provided it is not too big, is a very reasonable test to include (at a distance of 3.60 m/12 ft) as it is something you might well have to jump out hunting.

I would like to end this chapter where I started by reiterating that a good hunter, horse or pony, should get round the course and do so freely and well. Otherwise it is not a good course.

12 ◇ *Planning and Setting up a Course*

Before he sets to work on his design for a course the course designer will obtain the following information:

- The exact dimensions of the arena.
- The location of any permanent obstacles and natural features.
- The position of the entrance.
- The position of the judges' box.
- The position of the members' and public stands.
- The position of the afternoon sun.
- A list of fences and material.
- The timetable of competitions.
- The number of entries and likely starters in each competition.
- Details of the arena party who will be building the courses.

Having obtained these, the course designer's first task then is to make a plan of the arena to scale.

This is easily done using graph paper. Everything that is marked on the plan must be drawn to scale and this particularly applies to the fences. Don't forget that if you use poles of a certain length you must add the width of any wings when drawing fences on the plan.

This is especially important in small arenas and indoors, and helps to avoid discovering on the ground that one fence interferes with the horses' approach to another.

The plan of the course must show:

- The position of the start and finish.
- The fences, their type, numbers and the direction in which they are jumped.
- Any compulsory passages or turning points.
- The length of the course as measured.
- The rules under which the competition is judged.
- The time allowed and time limit.
- The obstacles to be used in any jump-off as well as the length of the course, time allowed and time limit.
- Any combinations that are to be judged as closed or as partially closed.

Course plans must be issued to:

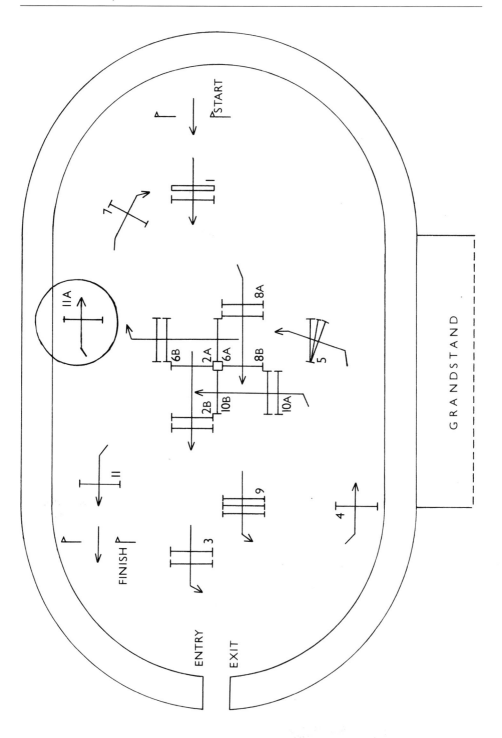

- The judges (two copies).
- The commentator.
- The collecting ring.
- The chief arena steward.
- Section heads of the arena party.
- Television or radio commentators (if applicable).

With the plans for the commentators and the arena party should go a description of the fences, similar to some of those shown in this book. Ideally, each arena party section head and the chief arena steward should be provided with a folder of the course plans – each one in a clear plastic envelope with the plan on one side and the descriptions on the reverse.

The chief arena steward is the course designer's right-hand man. Ideally he is a qualified course designer himself. His task is to control the activities of his arena party throughout the show and to see that the wishes of the course designer are efficiently carried out.

I love a course that is logical and easy for spectators to follow. When you have finished setting up your course, look at it from a spectator's vantage point to check that it fills the arena and satisfies the eye. It is fun, especially in a speed class, to have a geometric feature as a centrepiece and an example of this, in the form of a swastica, is shown as Fig. 44.

Now with the course plans prepared and the jumping equipment ready, the course designer arrives at the ground. The first thing is to establish a good working relationship with the chief arena steward and the arena party and to brief them on what is required. Different course designers use different terms to describe certain items of equipment, so before anything else is done everyone must agree on the terms that will be used.

Once the course designer has got to know his team and established agreed terminology, he will ask his chief arena steward to divide the arena party into two or three teams or sections of four people, each with a section leader who has a copy of the course plan. The chief arena steward works independently, as does the course designer, and both of them require two helpers to carry equipment and material.

The course designer will start siting his fences by first of all setting down poles and numbers. The poles mark exactly the front and back elements of the fence. The chief arena steward, using his description of the fences, will now arrange for the right material to be brought to the spot by one section who will start to build that fence. Once the first fence is exactly sited the course designer marks the exact position of the next and the second section starts to build it. This process continues

Fig. 44 *Table C. Jump-off fences: 1, 2, 6, 8, 10, 11. Course with a geometric centrepiece. Note: Fence 11 would be better sited where 11A is shown. But this would take much longer, as horses turn away from the entrance. If each horse took an extra 30 seconds and there were 60 in the class you would lose half an hour just on this small consideration.*

with the sections leapfrogging one another until the course is set. The chief follows behind to dress the fences with flags, shrubs and so on and checks the measurements of each from the course plan. It is a good idea if he also has wedges of wood to make sure that the fences are straight, horizontal and firmly based. By the time the course designer has reached the end of his course, the first fence will be ready for his final inspection and decisions with regard to any alterations.

Never be afraid to make a change if you see that it would improve the course. There is more skill in the actual siting and presentation of the fences than in planning. I have permission to quote from the translation of an *aide memoire*, dated February, 1962, and produced for the FEI by Col. de Brothonne and Mr. G. de Ybarra. They said: '. . . he must have time to construct his course in peace. In a big show, when several courses have to be prepared, the course builder must have half a day. In a smaller show, except for courses for the first day which must be prepared the day before, the course builder should have, during the morning of each day of the show, a minimum of $3\frac{1}{2}$ hours provided his assistants are competent, sufficiently numerous and energetic. Competitions run in the morning are always to the detriment of the quality of the show. A system which consists of preparing a course on paper in minute detail and then reproducing it slavishly on the ground leads always to trouble.' Those were the days.

These are idealistic arrangements and we are not often able to enjoy such circumstances, but the theory is absolutely right.

Someone asked me recently why I thought that literally thousands of people sit for hours to watch the final show jumping phase of the three-day events at Badminton and Burghley. After all, they rightly said, the standard, by true show jumping standards, is very low, and yet people who wouldn't cross the road to see a good show jumping competition pack the stands for this. Why?

On reflection perhaps it was because these courses are built in the way recommended all those years ago by the FEI. Endless time and trouble have been taken to make the arena a work of art worthy of a great occasion. The genius, always applied to the cross-country course, is also put into the show jumping with predictable results.

While the course designer is going round on his final inspection, the chief arena steward and the sections assemble material for subsequent classes. The course designer may want to build some of them now and close them off by crossing their flags in front of the fence. A balance must be struck between the need to save time between competitions and the danger of cluttering up the arena. Too many fences that are not a part of the course that is being jumped can destroy the logic of the course for spectators, as well as detracting from the beauty of the arena.

However, equipment for building new fences in later competitions must be assembled in sets that are complete so that when they are put up there is no unnecessary delay. Spare equipment must be located as close as possible to that which it is to replace and not on the opposite side of the arena. Responsibility for the unobtrusive stacking of spare material must be allocated, for the whole appearance of the arena can be spoiled by untidy equipment. Above all, it must not be put in front of sponsors' sign boards.

Now that the course is ready its length can be measured, and much controversy can be avoided if this is done correctly. The line to be measured is that which is 'normally followed by the horse' (FEI Regulations, Article 204.1). It is the course designer's responsibility to give a correct measurement to the judges. If he is going to allow a senior steward to measure for him he ought to check the first course on each day of the show by measuring it himself and ensuring that there is no discrepancy. The course for the jump-off must also be measured and marked on all the course plans before the competition starts.

When the course is completely ready, the chief arena steward will allocate duties to the arena party section leaders and tell them when they must be on duty and when they can rest. Sections must stay together during the show and their leaders must control the movements of their men. If control is lost the efficiency of the whole team is greatly impaired and delays to the timetable become inevitable.

13 ◇ *International Course Designers and Their Courses*

The course plans that follow are fascinating for the insight that they give to the differences of approach, personality and method of each of these talented individuals. I have submitted them as they were sent to me, where appropriate with extracts from the letters of those concerned.

ALAN BALL

We start with Alan Ball, for many years the senior course designer of the BSJA. Since the untimely death of John Gross in 1968 on the return journey from the Royal Cornwall Show, Alan has been Britain's top course designer. His home was Southport, Lancashire, whence his brother John built very good courses all around the north west of the country.

Photo 53 *Alan Ball in action at Olympia, 1990.*

OPPOSITE: **Fig. 45** *Class 75 Midland Bank Championships King George V Gold Cup Table A Article 238.3.AM4, designed by Alan Ball.*

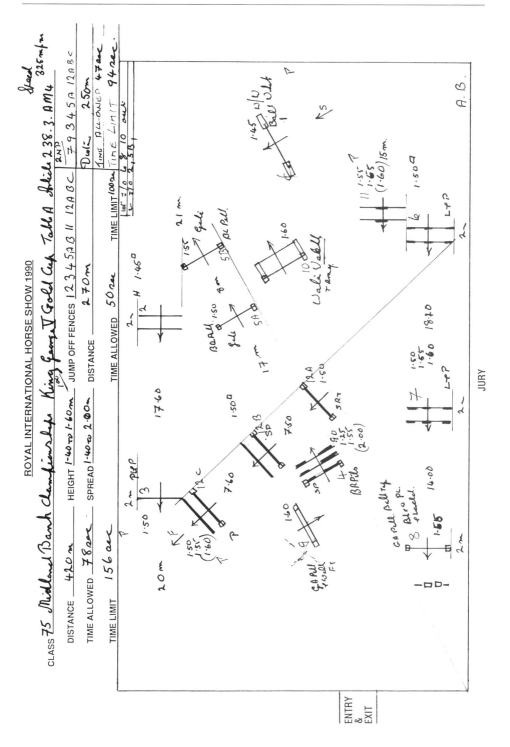

ROYAL INTERNATIONAL HORSE SHOW 1990

CLASS 75 Midland Bank Championship King George V Gold Cup Table A Article 238.3. AM4 325 m/m

Good

DISTANCE 420 m   HEIGHT 1·40 to 1·60m   JUMP OFF FENCES 1 2 3 4 5 A B 11 12 A B C   ₇ 9 3 4 5 A 12 A B C

TIME ALLOWED 78 sec   SPREAD 1·40 to 2·00m   DISTANCE 270m   2ND   250m

TIME LIMIT 156 sec   TIME ALLOWED 50 sec   DISTANCE 1000m   Time Allowed 47sec

TIME LIMIT 94 sec

JURY

A.B.

ENTRY
&
EXIT

Alan must, I guess, have built more courses in more countries than anyone else. He is famous for his organisation of the arena. At the great London shows, building the course during the interval from an empty arena has to be completed in twelve minutes. There are plenty of people for whom this is one of the highlights of the show. As the band strikes up, the tractors drive in with the material for each fence carefully loaded. Four top designers/builders are each responsible for one of the four quarters (or corners as they are known) of the arena. For about five minutes it looks like bedlam, except that Alan is never seen to be in a hurry, and then suddenly there is a marvellous course with the flower decorators putting the finishing touches.

The course in Fig. 45 is one that Alan set for the King George V Gold Cup in 1990. On the copies issued at the show the fences are coloured so that everyone knows which ones to use. Note the famous 'cabbage lines' which are laid down before the fences on the diagonals are started. I guess that 12A would be the first one built once the lines were down.

PAMELA CARRUTHERS

Pamela Carruthers is a name that is synonymous with the Hickstead Derby. She built that course – probably the most famous course in the world – in 1960 and in the first twenty-one years she achieved the extraordinary record of twenty-one clear rounds. What is more, she developed an uncanny knack of picking the

Photo 54 *Jon Doney, Pam Carruthers' successor at Hickstead, at work in the unique and beautiful arena.*

Photo 55 *A daunting prospect – the Devil's Dyke. Hollow and 1.40 m (4 ft 6 ins) high, the slope is pretty steep. Even momentary hesitation by the horse makes faults inevitable.*

Photo 56 *Width is a feature of Hickstead's magnificent fences.*

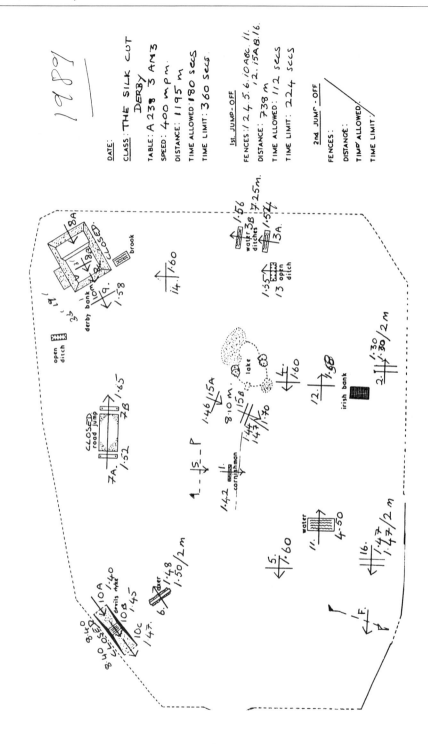

1989

DATE:

CLASS: THE SILK CUT
DERBY

TABLE: A 238 3 AM 3

SPEED: 400 m p m

DISTANCE: 1195 m

TIME ALLOWED: 180 secs

TIME LIMIT: 360 secs

1st JUMP - OFF

FENCES: 1. 2. 4. 5. 6. 10 A&c. 11.
12. 15 A&.16.

DISTANCE: 738 m

TIME ALLOWED: 112 secs

TIME LIMIT: 224 secs

2nd JUMP - OFF

FENCES:

DISTANCE:

TIME ALLOWED:

TIME LIMIT:

winner before the event.

Pam was an international rider herself in the years after the war. She has travelled the world and is one of the most highly respected figures in show jumping. She is still in demand at Spruce Meadows, Calgary, where she helped to get that great show going in the early days. She has handed the reins at Hickstead to Jon Doney now, and is proud to watch his great success there and elsewhere.

The two most famous Hickstead Derby fences are the Bank with a vertical fence of short white planks 1.58 m (5 ft 2 ins) high placed 10 m (33 ft) from the base of the bank; and, of course, the Devil's Dyke (Photo 55). But all the great fences on this 1195 m (1300 yd) course take their toll and many high hopes have been dashed at the final Silver Birch Oxer with its huge 2 m (6 ft 6 ins) spread. There are twenty-three efforts on the course.

Fig. 46 *All England Jumping Course – International Arena.*

1	*Stone wall*
2	*3 flights of white rails*
3A & B	*White rails on back of ditch*
4	*Gate and rail*
5	*Wall*
6	*White rails and hedge*
7	*Road jump*
8A	*Bank*
8B	*White rails, 3 flights*
8C	*Face of bank*
9	*3 flights of white rails*
10A	*Devil's Dyke rustic rails*
10B	*Rustic rails and ditch*
10C	*Rustic rails*
11	*Open water*
12	*Palisade*
13	*Rustic rails on back of ditch*
14	*Balustrade*
15A	*Gate*
15B	*Gate and rail*
16	*3 flights of rustic rails*

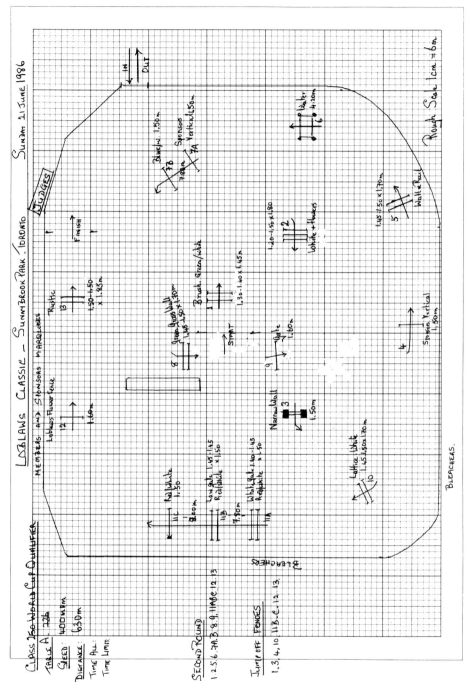

Fig. 47 *Christopher Coldrey's design for the Loblaws Classic, Toronto, 1986.*

CHRISTOPHER COLDREY

The course shown opposite was a big one – worthy of the brilliant Canadian show jumpers. Every fence caused faults at least once, so the course demanded concentration from start to finish. The double of verticals after the water was brilliantly jumped. Riders had to get their horses balanced and collected after extending over the water, without losing the impulsion needed for these two big efforts. The slightly uphill approach to the treble combination made it more difficult than it appeared. The last fence needed decisive riding and produced some marvellous leaps.

JON DONEY

Jon Doney started course designing at the early age of thirteen and is now designing courses worldwide. Jon's interest in course building was first kindled when travelling the country with his family, who were deeply involved with show jumping and racing. When time permitted he hunted with the Duke of Beaufort's hounds in Gloucestershire. Upon leaving school he joined his father's business in the west of England, but in time, the lures of competition brought him back into the sport.

It was in 1966 that he first built at the Ascot Festival, which led to invitations to work at Hickstead and many other leading shows around the country, and to his eventual appointment to the National Course Builders' Panel in the late 1960s.

In 1976 Jon joined the British Show Jumping Association as one of their Senior Course Designers, and is now responsible for the National Course Designers' appointments.

In 1978 he was appointed to the FEI Course Designers' Panel and has since built in twenty-three different countries worldwide. For the last three years he has designed the course for the world's largest prize-money competition at Spruce Meadows in Canada.

In 1989 Jon took over as the Senior Course Designer at Hickstead.

In 1988 the FEI chose twelve leading experts from all over the world to form a specialist panel to lecture and test future international officials. Jon was appointed to this list on its inception, and, with Pamela Carruthers, was instrumental in writing the special FEI Course Designers' Test Papers.

As we've seen earlier in the book, Jon is also the course designer at the Badminton Horse Trials and some examples of his work there are shown in Chapter 10.

TED DWYER

Ted Dwyer lives in Young, New South Wales, Australia with his wife Judy and sons, Timothy and Brendan. Together they run Ellmore, a 1600-acre mixed farm which has been in the family for four generations.

Ted's first interest in show jumping was as the owner of Ocean Foam, one of the top horses in Australia from 1958–1969. Ridden by Kevin Bacon, Ocean Foam represented Australia at the Olympic Games in Tokyo in 1964.

Ted has been building courses since 1957 and joined the international panel in 1980. He has built courses and conducted seminars throughout Australia and in New Zealand, Singapore, Hong Kong and Manila. He became an international judge in 1984.

He organised Australia's leading international show at Wentworth Park, Sydney from 1979–87, doing much to promote show jumping in Australia by bringing out teams from the UK, Canada, USA, Italy, Switzerland, New Zealand, Ireland, etc. At Max Amman's suggestion Ted began the Pacific League of the World Cup in 1979 and has been its co-ordinator ever since. His contribution to Australian show jumping, both as an organiser and a course designer, has been a major factor in his country's rise to the highest level in this sport.

Ted Dwyer says:

> 'The enclosed copy of the course plan was of the World Cup Pacific League qualifier at Canberra A.C.T.Aust. on Jan. 28th 1989. On the plan are the various dimensions of the fences. I set out to produce a course that tested the horse for scope and ability; the fences were big and wide with ample room to get to them. I wished to test the rider with a number of lines from the double to fence 5, from fence 6 to 7 and from fence 10 to the treble. A number of the fences were off corners.
>
> '31 horses started in the Class and in the first round 11 horses were clear with 4 on four faults. 17 of the leading horses started in the second round and of these 6 were clear with 5 on four faults. The jump-off against the clock was over a course that now had a number of the verticals at the maximum of 1.60 m, with spreads to 1.80 m and 2.10 m on the triple bar. Five horses contested the final barrage and of these 3 went clear with less than three seconds dividing the horses. A very satisfying competition which was a very good crowd pleaser. The horses that contested the final round all had scope and ability and it came down to the winners who had all of these qualities.'

OPPOSITE: **Fig. 48** *Ted Dwyer's course plan for the World Cup Pacific League qualifier, Canberra.*

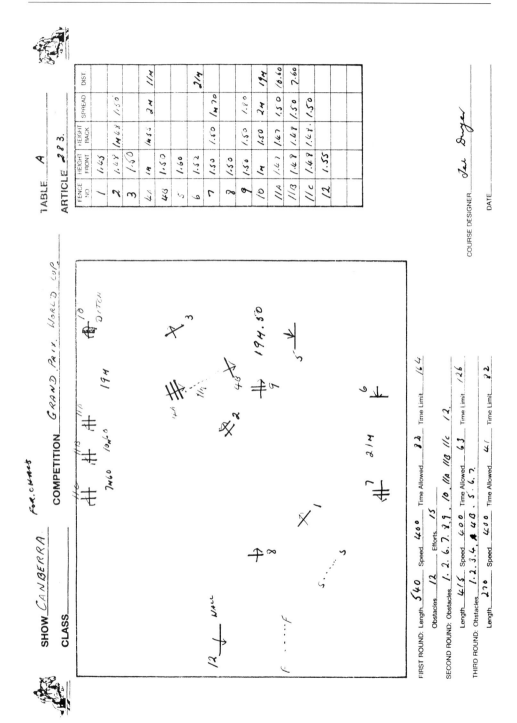

SHOW _CANBERRA_

COMPETITION _GRAND PRIX. WORLD CUP_

CLASS

TABLE _A_

ARTICLE _283._

FOR CHASE

FENCE NO	HEIGHT FRONT	HEIGHT BACK	SPREAD	DIST
1	1.45			
2	1.48	1.48	1.50	
3	1.50			
4A	1M	1M55	2M	1M
4B	1.50			
5	1.60			
6	1.52			2M
7	1.50	1.50	1M70	
8	1.50			
9	1.50	1.50	1.80	1M
10	1M	1.50	2M	1M
11A	1.47	1.47	1.50	10.60
11B	1.48	1.48	1.50	7.60
11C	1.48	1.48	1.50	
12	1.55			

COURSE DESIGNER _Jac Dugen_

DATE

FIRST ROUND: Length _540_ Speed _400_ Time Allowed _82_ Time Limit _164_

Obstacles _12_ Efforts. _15_ Obstacles _1. 2. 6. 7. 8. 9. 10. 11A 11B 11C 12._

SECOND ROUND: Length _615_ Speed _600_ Time Allowed _63_ Time limit _126_

Obstacles _1. 2. 3. 4. 4B. 5. 6. 7._

THIRD ROUND: Length _270_ Speed _600_ Time Allowed _41_ Time Limit _82_

Photo 57   *Ted Dwyer* (left) *with the author, at the Royal Sydney Show.*

ARNO GEGO

Arno Gego is best known as course designer for the CSIO, Aachen. He was a student of Hans-Heinrich Brinkman, both as a successful rider of the top grade, and as 'Parcours chef'. Arno is chairman of the International Course Designers' Council, has been the technical delegate at championships world-wide, including Olympic Games, World Championships and World Cup, and has built courses just about everywhere that there is show jumping. He is a distinguished engineer, an honorary Professor of Agricultural Engineering, and a director of Klöcken-Humboldt-Deutz AG, Cologne. He is married, with two sons and speaks five languages. Arno is a very interesting man with whom to discuss every aspect of course designing, being a great thinker as well as a world-famous exponent of his art.

Arno Gego says:

> 'I gladly accept the invitation to present an example of a satisfying course. I think as course designer of CSIO Aachen, I should not present a course of Mexico, Venezuela or Australia, but one course from the annual CSIO, Aachen. In addition I selected a quite normal class without exceptional tasks

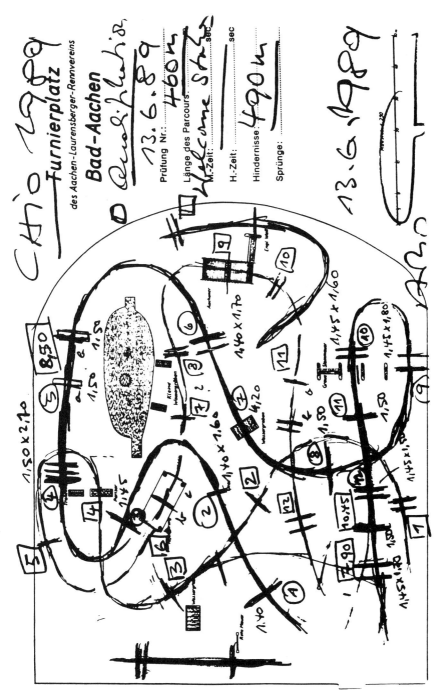

Fig. 49 One of Arno Gego's Aachen course designs.

with double Liverpool or similar in order to prevent undesirable copying.

'The first Grand Prix of the annual CSIO Aachen is the "Internationales Springchampionat der Bundesrepublik Deutschland" on Wednesday afternoon. Exactly 30 participants are allowed to enter, qualified by only one previous class: the first 1.50 m competition on Tuesday afternoon. Normally 80 to 90 participants from 12 to 15 nations, the world-wide best horses and riders, are competing: Table A on time, maximum 1.50 m and 400 m/min. are the conditions.

'So this competition is asking to meet different interests:

1. Please the crowd and serve the whole big arena (125 m × 150 m).
2. Consider that this class is the first competition for each participating horse.
3. Be sure not to have more than 30 horses to be clear.
4. Provide an inviting starting line.
5. Try to select the 30 best horses.
6. Make sure not to overdemand the field of competitors.
7. Again, please the crowd and produce a fast and big Table A class.

'My proposition for this class was the presented Masterplan (numbers in circle) with the following concept characteristics:

1. Easy and inviting starting line (1, 2, 3) with modest dimensions.
2. First selecting line (4, 5A, B) close to the second Main Tribune.
3. Strong finishing line (10, 11, 12A, B, C) in front of the Main Tribune, more difficult by distance than by dimension.
4. Connecting the two straight lines from 5B to 10 by generous and swinging line and integrating a 4.20 m water jump.
5. Having only five 1.50 m obstacles.
6. Filling the arena and still having a length of the course below 500 m in the big Aachen arena.
7. Getting 22 clears (25%) with needed times between 62.30 and 73.60 seconds (4 seconds between first and fifth). 62 competitors with not more than 8 faults (87 starters totally).
8. Only 3 horses eliminated or retired.
9. A total amount of 487.75 points with 84 finishing starters led to 5.8 points/competitor, which is 1.45 knock-down per starter.
10. The decision about the result of each competitor was open to the very last fence (12C). It was a fast class!

'The reader should consider best grass-ground conditions (grippy and elastic footing) and best horses. During the CSIO Aachen 1989 there was only fine weather with 24–28°C, only sun and no rain! The ground was irrigated each night.'

BERTALAN DE NEMETHY

Bertalan de Nemethy was coach to the United States Equestrian Jumping Team Squad from 1955 to 1980. During this time he led his squad from nothing to the best in the world. He demanded perfection from his riders and never accepted less than the best as a course designer.

A former Hungarian cavalry officer and riding instructor at the Royal Hungarian Cavalry School, he was a member of the Hungarian Olympic Squad for the 1940 Games, which were cancelled by the outbreak of World War II. After working as a trainer in Denmark after the war, de Nemethy came to the United States in 1952 and became a citizen in 1958.

Although 'Bert' de Nemethy never did get to the Games as a rider, he has coached six US Olympic Teams, five Pan-American Games Teams, and four World Championship Teams.

His teams won the Olympic silver medal in 1960 in Rome and 1972 in Munich. They also won the gold medals in the 1959, 1963, 1975, and 1979 Pan-American Games, and individual gold medals were won by Mary Mairs Chapot in 1963 and Michael Matz in 1979.

One of his riders, William Steinkraus, became the first American equestrian to win an individual Olympic gold medal (1968, Mexico City). Another de Nemethy coached rider, Neal Shapiro, won the individual bronze medal at the 1972 Munich Games, and Joe Fargis took the individual gold medal at the 1984 Los Angeles Olympics.

In the 1974 World Championships at Hickstead, Frank Chapot tied for the individual bronze medal, and in 1978 Aachen, the USET won the team bronze and Michael Matz the individual bronze medal.

His teams competed in 144 Nations' Cups, winning 71 and taking second place 36 times. His individual riders won 72 international Grand Prix competitions, 44 team championships, and over 400 international classes all over the world.

De Nemethy designed the jumping courses at the Los Angeles Olympics in 1984, and the 1980 and 1989 World Cup Finals in Baltimore and Tampa respectively.

Bert de Nemethy says:

> 'Enclosed you will find photocopies of my World Cup Final courses in Tampa, Florida, 1989. All three courses were designed in accordance with my principles. All obstacles were newly designed and never jumped before by anybody.
>
> 'They were gradually introduced, and by the Final's third competition all of the obstacles had been jumped in a different position, as well as all the distances between the fences. The courses were balanced, as you can see evenly spread throughout the arena. All three finish lines were close to the out gate to save time; on the other hand, the position of the starting lines gave the riders a chance to go around and between the obstacles, making familiar the place for the horses.

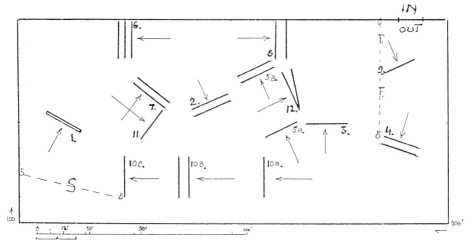

F.E.J. TAB. C., ART. 239,268,658,2,3.
RULES WORLD CUP FORMULA 6TH EDITION
12 OBSTACLES
SPEED: 350m/min.
LENGTH OF COURSE: _____
TIME ALLOWED: _____
TIME LIMIT: _____

VOLVO WORLD CUP FINAL
FIRST COMPETITION

Presented by Budweiser
(No Jump Off)

WEDNESDAY, APRIL 12, 1989
7:30 P.M.

V.W. CUP COMPETITION.

FIRST COMPETITION
T.H.B.C. - NO JUMP OFF.

NO. OF FENCE	HIGHT	SPRED	NO OF FENCE	HIGHT	SPRED
	M.	M.		M.	M.
1.	WALL 1.35		8.	OXER 1.45 - 1.45	1.60
2.	OXER 1.45 - 1.50	1.20	9.	UPRIGHT 1.50	
3.	UPRIGHT 1.50		10.A.	UPRIGHT 1.45	
4.	OXER 1.40 - 1.45	1.50	10.B.	OXER 1.40 - 1.45	1.50
5.A	UPRIGHT 1.45		10.C.	UPRIGHT 1.50	
5.B	OXER 1.50 - 1.50	1.40	11.	UPRIGHT 1.55	
6.	TRIPLE BAR 0.55 -1.55	2.00	12.	FAN 1.45 to CENTER	2.00 H CN OUTSIDE
7.	OXER 1.35 - 1.35	1.65			

Figs 50–52 *Three World Cup final courses from Tampa, Florida, designed by Bertalan de Nemethy.*

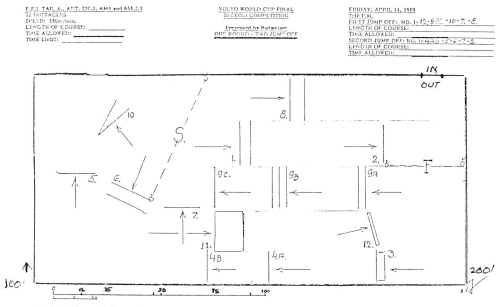

F.E.I. TAB. A., ART. 238.3, AM1 and 658.2.3
12 OBSTACLES
SPEED: 350m/min.
LENGTH OF COURSE: _____
TIME ALLOWED: _____
TIME LIMIT: _____

VOLVO WORLD CUP FINAL
SECOND COMPETITION

Presented by Budweiser
ONE ROUND - TWO JUMP OFF

FRIDAY, APRIL 14, 1989
7:30 P.M.
FIRST JUMP OFF: NO. 1- 12, 9B, -10 - 7, - 8.
LENGTH OF COURSE:
TIME ALLOWED:
SECOND JUMP OFF: NO. 1- 4B, - 5 - 6 - 7 - 8.
LENGTH OF COURSE:
TIME ALLOWED:

V. W. CUP COMPETITION

SECOND COMPETITION

NO. OF FENCE	HIGHT	SPRED	NO. OF FENCE	HIGHT	SPRED
1.	1.35 - 1.45	1.50	8.	OXER 1.55 - 1.55	1.70
2.	UPRIGHT 1.50		9. A	OXER 1.45 - 1.45	1.50
3.	OXER - OVERPOOL 1.45	1.50	9. B	TRIPLE BAR 0.60 - 1.55	1.60
4. A	UPRIGHT 1.55		9. C	UPRIGHT 1.60	
4. B	UPRIGHT 1.50		10.	FAN 1.45 IN MIDDLE	
5.	UPRIGHT 1.55		11.	WATER 1.50	UPRIGHT 2.20
6.	OXER 1.50 - 1.50	1.55	12.	WALL 1.60	
7.	UPRIGHT 1.60				

Fig. 51

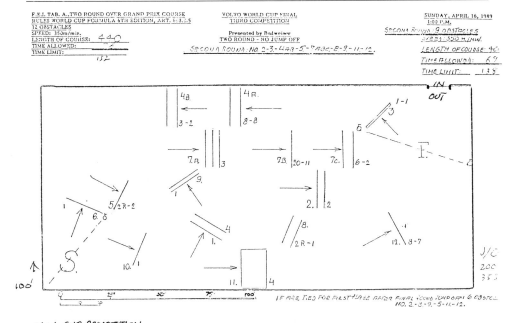

F.E.I. TAB. A., TWO ROUND OVER GRAND PRIX COURSE
RULES WORLD CUP FORMULA 6TH EDITION, ART. 6:3.2.5
12 OBSTACLES
SPEED: 350m/min.
LENGTH OF COURSE: 440
TIME ALLOWED:
TIME LIMIT:
152

VOLVO WORLD CUP FINAL
THIRD COMPETITION

Presented by Budweiser
TWO ROUND - NO JUMP OFF

SECOND ROUND: NO. 2-3-4A-5-7A3C-8-9-11-12.

SUNDAY, APRIL 16, 1989
1:00 P.M.
SECOND ROUND: 9 OBSTACLES
SPEED: 350 M/MIN.
LENGTH OF COURSE: 96
TIME ALLOWED: 67
TIME LIMIT: 135

IF ARE TIED FOR FIRST PHASE AFTER FINAL ROUND JUMP OFF: 6 OBSTCL.
NO. 2-8-9-5-11-12.

V. W. CUP COMPETITION
THIRD - COMPETITION

NO. OF FENCE	HEIGHT	SPREAD	NO. OF FENCE	HEIGHT	SPREAD
1.	1.40 - 1.40	1.50	7c.	1.50 - 1.50	1.60
2.	1.45 - 1.45	1.60	8.	1.40 - 1.45	1.60
3.	1.60		9.	1.60	
4 (A)	1.45 - 1.50	1.55	10	1.50	
4 (B)	1.50 - 1.50	1.55	11.	WATER 1.50	3.00
5.	1.55		12.	1.60	
6.	1.50				
7 (A)	TRIPLE BAR 0.40 - 1.55 LIVERPOOL				
7 (B)	1.50				

Fig. 52

'The distances used between the fences required the most experience and judgment from the riders and best training of the horses. All fences were knocked down and no accident happened.

'The construction of the obstacles was carefully designed to avoid injury for riders and horses (3 rails were broken during the entire Final's competition).

'It is my principle not to disclose officially the distances between obstacles. Riders, trainers, as well as the media have the time for inspection and they should use their judgment. To make public the related distances can be dangerous, if they will be used at other places, and under other circumstances by less experienced riders and horses.'

STEVE HICKEY

Steve Hickey served in the Irish Army from 1942 until his retirement in 1984. He travelled abroad with the Army Jumping Team for sixteen years. On promotion to Sgt Major he was responsible for the erection of all courses for the schooling of horses. In this he was able to follow the progress of young horses from negotiating a pole on the ground to their eventual participation in international events.

Steve is still actively designing courses, having built at the Royal Easter Show in Sydney, lots of venues around Ireland and, of course, the RDS Horse Show.

Steve Hickey says:

'The enclosed course [shown overleaf] I regard as one of my best.

'It was the second Championship Competition (Final Team and Second Individual) in the 1982 World Show Jumping Championship held in Dublin. There were 53 competitors, with only one Double Clear Round, the great French horse Flambeau C, with Frederic Cottier his rider. The very good Belgian horse Cyrano, ridden by Edgar-Henri Cuepper, was also clear jumping but incurred one and three quarters time faults.

'What pleased me most was the fact that, while very demanding and difficult, I got almost 99% around, no one got 'hung up' and no injuries. As a matter of fact, not one pole was broken for the whole Championship.

'I would sum up in this way:

1. Demanding but jumpable, with no artificially created problems or extreme difficulties.
2. Combination – difficult while at the same time I wanted to avoid eliminations and give the horses a fair chance.
3. For all the participants to have a sense of achievement and at the end a worthy champion.'

WORLD SHOWJUMPING CHAMPIONSHIP — DUBLIN : 1982

DATE 10th JUNE | TIME 9:00 am & 2:00 p.m. (7 cards) | COMP No.5 | TABLE A

ART. NO. 238.7, A7; E 283.B 3(a); 283.B.3.b.(1)

LEN OF COURSE 660 H | SPEED 400 M. per Min | TIME ALLOWED 99 sec. / 198 sec.

LEN OF COURSE 3tcn

JUMP OFF (IF REQUIRED) FENCE NOS. 1, 10a,b, 11, 12, 13, & 14.

JURY

NO.	TYPE	FENCE DESCRIPTION	HEIGHT FRONT	HEIGHT BACK	SPREAD
1.	P	BLACK & AMBER	1.43	1.50	1.50
2.	P	BLUE, WHITE & GREEN	1.46	1.48	1.60
3.	U	WISHING WELL, BLUE & SAFFRON POLES	1.56		1.80
4.	P	VIADUCT WALLS WITH YELLOW POLES	1.50	1.52	1.80
5.	U	O'CONNELL BRIDGE 23.00	1.60		
6a.	P	GREEN & WHITE	1.45	1.55	1.70
6b.	P	GREEN & WHITE 7.60 H.	1.48	1.50	1.70
7.	S	WATER	.90		4.50
8.	S	TRIPLE BAR F.E.I. COLOURS	1.36	1.54	2.00

P - PARALLEL   U - UPRIGHT   S - SPREAD

NO.	TYPE	FENCE DESCRIPTION	HEIGHT FRONT	HEIGHT BACK	SPREAD
9.	U	BLUE PARK GATE, GREY PILLARS 22.4CM.	1.50		
10a	U	RED & WHITE GEORGIAN DOORS 7.77 M.	1.50		
10b	P	RED & WHITE PICKET & POLES 7.60 M.	1.47	1.50	1.75
10c	P	RED & WHITE POLES	1.52	1.55	1.80
11.	U	R.D.S. CLOCK TOWERS, BLACK & WHITE	1.60		
12.	P	MERRION GATES WITH POLE	1.53	1.55	1.90
13.	U	TOWERS, RUSTIC WALL & POLES	1.56		
14.	P	BLUE & WHITE POLES OVER WATER	1.49	1.54	2.00

N.B. POSITIONS OF FENCES ARE APPROXIMATE

HAROLD PRESTON

Harold Preston started course designing about thirty years ago and has been on the FEI International Course Designers' Panel and the FEI International Judges' Panel for many years. He is, and has been for about eighteen years, a member of the South African National Equestrian Federation Management Committee, and Chairman of the National Show Jumping Committee. He has been invited to design courses and judge in several countries and has on many occasions been the course designer for all South Africa's major events, Grand Prix, and championships.

Harold's courses have been instrumental in bringing and keeping South African show jumpers amongst the best in the world. When sporting ties resume with the rest of the world his country will owe him a great debt.

Harold Preston says:

'The enclosed course was, I think, a successful one and most of the riders

ABOVE: **Photo 58**   *Harold Preston at work.*

LEFT: **Fig. 53**   *Steve Hickey's World Championship course from Dublin, 1982.*

THE ROYAL AGRICULTURAL SOCIETY OF NATAL

DATE	Friday 25 May 1990
TIME	14.00
CLASS	44 (i)
GRADE	A
TABLE	AM3

FIRST ROUND		
LENGTH	610	M
SPEED	400	MPM
TIME ALLO.	92	SECS
TIME LIMIT	184	SECS

JUMP OFF		
JUMPS	1-2-3-9-10BC-11-12	
LENGTH	360	M
TIME ALLO.	54	SEC
TIME LIMIT	108	SEC

The Royal Grade A Grand Prix

1 Oxer   4'7½"/4'9"/5'0"
2 Vertical   4'11"
3 Oxer   4'9"/4'9"/5'6"
4 Triple Bar   5'3"/6'6"
5A Vertical   5'0"
  B Vertical   5'1½"
6 Water   13'0"
7 Vertical   5'0"
8 Oxer over water 5'0"/5'0"/5'6"
9 Wall   5'6"
10A Oxer   4'10"/5'0"/5'6"
  B Oxer   4'10"/5'0"/5'6"
  C Vertical   5'2"
11 Vertical   5'3"
12 Oxer   5'0"/5'0"/5'6"

5A-5B 36'0" 11-12 66'0"
10A-10B 24'0" 10B-10C 26'0"

thought so. There were about 22 starters and 6 went clear and no eliminations. The very open oxer over the water ditch, the treble combination and the distance between fences 11 and 12 caused most of the problems. Although perhaps not clear on the plan, it was possible to get inside fence 8 in the jump-off when going from fence 3 to fence 9, and inside fence 11 when going from fence 9 to 10B, and the winners used these options.'

PAUL WEIER

Paul Weier is one of the most sought-after international course designers. Previously a colonel in the Swiss Army, he was a brilliant competitor in the Swiss team and is a fine instructor and lecturer. His wife, Monica (née Bachmann), has also been a top international rider and is a famous teacher.

Paul is an intellectual course designer whose courses are technical, always interesting and often less easy than they look. He really makes riders think and they very much enjoy riding his tests. You can see from the following plans that Paul is a detailed and painstaking master of his craft who cares deeply about what happens in each competition.

Photo 59 *Paul Weier at Olympia in 1990, where he designed the course for the Volvo World Cup Qualifier (see Chapter 8).*

LEFT: **Fig. 54** *One of Harold Preston's Grand Prix courses from the Royal Agricultural Society, Natal.*

PAGES 138–144 **Figs 55–61** *A selection of Paul Weier's course plans.*

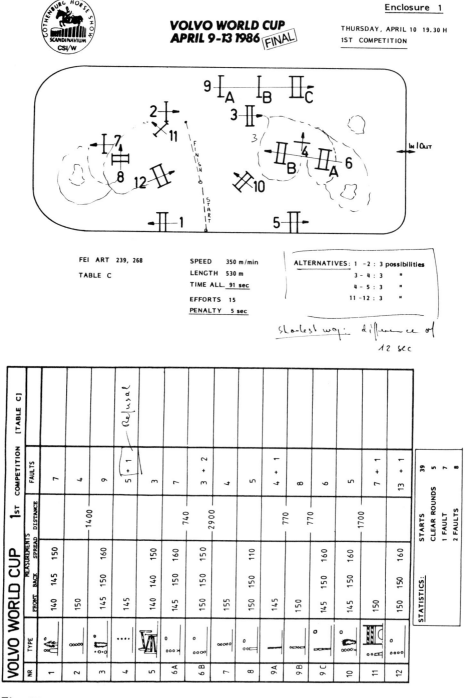

Fig. 55

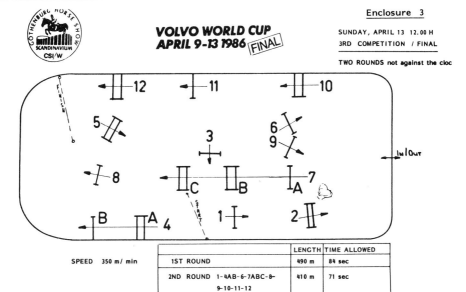

Fig. 56

EUROPEAN JUMPING CHAMPIONSHIP ST. GALLEN 1987

SPEED 400 M/MIN
LENGTH 700 m
TIME ALL 105 sec
EFFORTS 17
PENALTY 7 sec

TABLE C

STARTS	43
CLEAR ROUNDS	14
1 FAULT	12
2 FAULTS	7

1ST COMPETITION

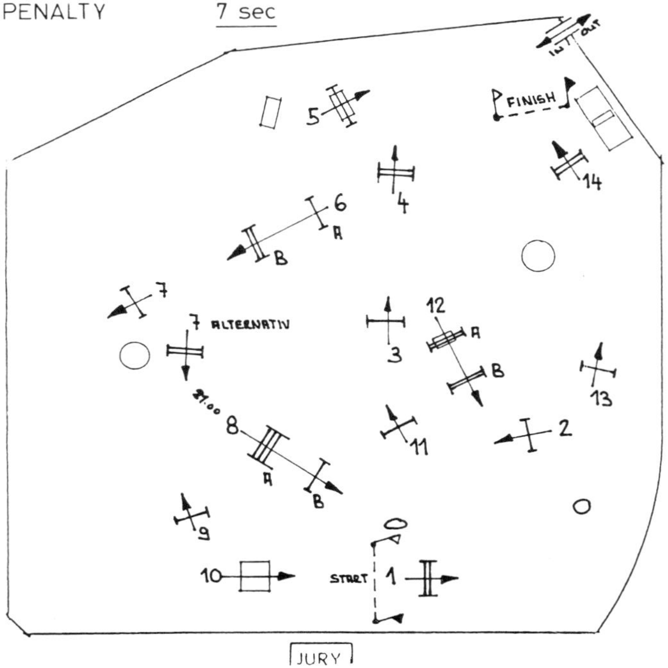

NR	TYPE	COLOUR	MEASUREMENTS FRONT	MEASUREMENTS BACK	MEASUREMENTS SPREAD	DISTANCE	FAULTS
1		green-red white	70	145	160		3
2		green-white	145				2
3		red-black yellow	150				1
4		green-white	140	150	160		2
5		rustic	150				4
6A		multicolour	145			7.60	1
6B		orange-black-white	140	145	150		7
7		white	150				2
7		nature	150	150	120		3
8A		red-white	90	140	200	8.00	1
8B		blue-white	150				4
9		birch	148				7
10		-			400		2
11		white red	150				1
12A		rustic	140	140	145	10.80	3
12B		rustic	145	150	130		5
13		green-white	150				4
14		red-black white	140	145	160		15

Fig, 57

EUROPEAN JUMPING CHAMPIONSHIP ST. GALLEN 1987

SPEED 400M/MIN
LENGTH 610 m
TIME ALL. 92 sec/95sec

JUMP OFF: 1-2-3-4-5-6AB

	1ST -	2ND ROUND
STARTS	43	33
CLEAR ROUNS	6	6
1 FAULT	7	2
2 FAULTS	8	7
TIME PENALTY	28	15

2ND COMPETITION NATIONS CUP

No	Type	Colour	Front	Back	Spread	Distance	Faults 1st Round	Faults 2nd Round
1		red-black white	140	145	140		0	3
2		blue-white	155				11	8
3		rustic	90	150	210		1	0
4		white-green-orange	155				6	7
5		white	150	150	150		14	10
6A		white-black orange	155			7.60	7	3
6B		white-black orange	148	155	160		5	5
7		—			430		1	3
8		green	155				16	15
9		autumn-birch	150	150	170		17	18
10		red-white	145	152	170		4	5
11		white-pol	160				5	4
12A		green-white	140	150	153	7.80	8	6
12B		green-white	152				4	4
12C		red-green white	150	155	150	10.70	12	3
13		blue	160				7	9

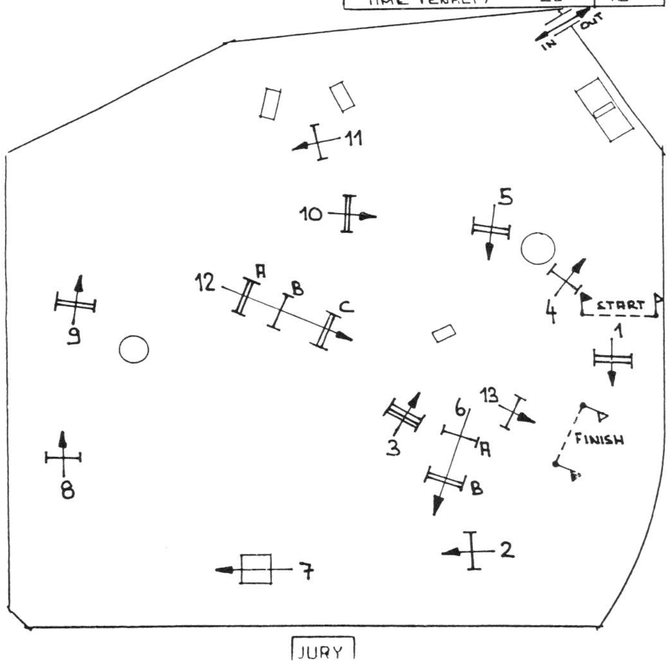

Fig. 58

EUROPEAN JUMPING CHAMPIONSHIP ST. GALLEN 1987

SPEED 400 M/MIN
LENGTH 530 m
TIME ALL. 80 sec

STARTS 20
CLEAR ROUNDS 3
1 FAULT 8
2 FAULTS 4

3 RD COMPETITION
ROUND A FINAL

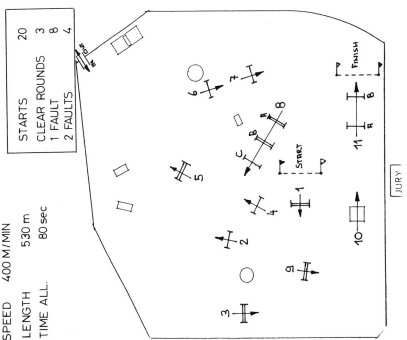

Nr.	Type	Colour	Front	Back	Speed	Distance	Faults
1		red-white	145	150	130		2
2		blue-yellow red	157				2
3		birch	150	155	160		3
4		white-blue	158				1
5		rustic	155	157	160		1
6		white red →	160			2000	−
7		white-black	160				−
8A		green-white orange	150	155	160	760	−
8B		green	152	152	160	780	5
8C		green-white	160				−
9		white	155	155	160		1
10		−			440	35m	−
11A		white-red	155				6
11B		white-red	160			780	4

Fig. 59

EUROPEAN JUMPING CHAMPIONSHIP ST.GALLEN 1987

SPEED 400 m/min
LENGTH 420 m
TIME ALL. 62 sec

STARTS 17
CLEAR ROUNDS 3
1 FAULT 6
2 FAULTS 7

3RD COMPETITION
ROUND B FINAL

Nr	TYPE	COLOUR	MEASUREMENTS Front	Back	Speed	DISTANCE	FAULTS
1		green-white-orange	150				–
2		blue-red white	155	160	160		3
3		rustic over water	80	155	200		–
4		white	160				8
5		red-white	150	155	165		3
6A		blue	150			1100	–
6B		blue-white	160			780	1
6C		blue	150	155	160		2
7		red-black white	152	157	170		5
8		rustic	160				–

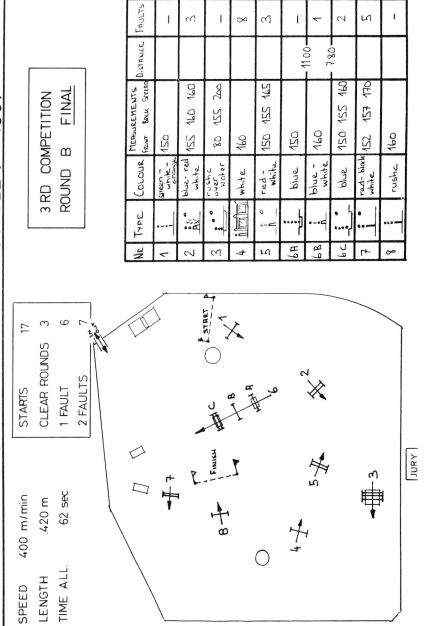

JURY

Fig. 60

EUROPEAN JUMPING CHAMPIONSHIP ST. GALLEN 1987

GRAND PRIX

SPEED 400 m/min

	1ST ROUND	2ND ROUND	JUMP OFF
LENGTH	550 m	490 m	250 m
TIME ALL.	83 sec	74 sec	38 sec

JUMP OFF: 1-3-4-6-7AB

STARTS	35	15
CLEAR ROUNDS	8	4
1 FAULT	11	7
2 FAULTS	8	4

TABLE A AGAINST THE CLOCK, TWO ROUNDS

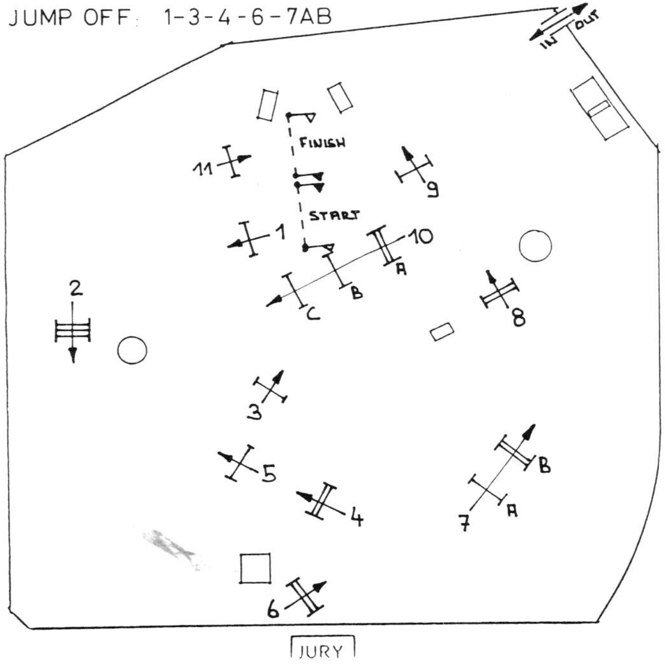

Nr.	Type	Colour	Measurements			Distance	Faults	
			Front	Back	Speed		1st Round & 2nd Round	2nd Round
1		rustic	145				—	—
2		blue-yellow-red	100	150	210		2	—
3		yellow-brown	155				1	—
4		green-white-red	150	155	160		2	3
5		white-green	155				1	✗
6		white-orange-blue	145	150	165		2	1
7A		autumn-colours	155				3	1
7B		autumn-colours	150	150	165	7.80	2	2
8		blue	150	155	150		4	✗
9		green	153				—	1
10A		white	150	155	160		3	1
10B		red-white	150			7.80	5	✗
10C		white	155			8.00	5	1
11		white-blue pole	160				12	6

JURY

Fig. 61

14 ◈ *Conclusion*

It has never been an objective of this book to tell anyone how to design a course, nor to be so dogmatic as to interfere with the individual style and flair of other course designers. A look through Chapter 13 will show how amazingly different are the drawings of the plans of these designers. Yet they were all chosen for supremacy in their field. Their courses are, in fact, just as different on the ground and I guess that most of us looking at a course set by any of the leading designers could say whose it was.

A good show jumper will jump anything provided that it is fair and reasonable. My purpose has been to put forward some facts, ideas and theories that might be helpful in the planning process. It is certain that we never stop learning about that marvellous animal, the horse, who in countless different fields so amply repays a lifetime of study. In the art and science of course building the same applies, as over the years we build on our own experience and that of others.

I hope that what comes through loud and clear is that you will never be a famous course designer unless you care deeply about your courses and what they look like. This means improving the material at your disposal if it is not good enough, even if you have to finish late at night and start early in the morning. It means, simply, not accepting anything third-rate or slapdash but insisting on proper back-up from show organisers. The most important factors, therefore, are hard work and meticulous planning, from the moment that you first sit down at the drawing board until you proudly announce the course 'open for inspection'.

Appendix A ◆ *Tables of Distances and Useful Conversions*

STRIDE CONVERSIONS

Single Strides
3 m   – (10 ft)
3.30 m – (11 ft)
3.60 m – (12 ft)
3.90 m – (13 ft)
4.20 m – (14 ft)

Related Distances
3 strides – 14.50 m – (48 ft)
4 strides – 18.00 m – (60 ft)
5 strides – 21.50 m – (72 ft)
6 strides – 25.00 m – (84 ft)
7 strides – 28.50 m – (96 ft)

DISTANCES IN COMBINATIONS

One Stride
7 m   – (23 ft)
7.10 m – (23 ft 3 ins)
7.20 m – (23 ft 6 ins)
7.30 m – (24 ft)
7.40 m – (24 ft 3 ins)
7.50 m – (24 ft 6 ins)
7.60 m – (25 ft)
7.70 m – (25 ft 3 ins)
7.80 m – (25 ft 6 ins)
7.90 m – (26 ft)
8.00 m – (26 ft 3 ins)
8.10 m – (26 ft 6 ins)
8.20 m – (27 ft)

Two Strides
10 m   – (33 ft)
10.10 m – (33 ft 3 ins)
10.20 m – (33 ft 6 ins)
10.30 m – (34 ft)
10.40 m – (34 ft 3 ins)
10.50 m – (34 ft 6 ins)
10.60 m – (35 ft)
10.70 m – (35 ft 3 ins)
10.80 m – (35 ft 6 ins)
10.90 m – (36 ft)
11.00 m – (36 ft 3 ins)
11.10 m – (36 ft 6 ins)
11.20 m – (37 ft)
11.30 m – (37 ft 3 ins)
11.40 m – (37 ft 6 ins)
11.50 m – (38 ft)
11.60 m – (38 ft 3 ins)
11.70 m – (38 ft 6 ins)
11.80 m – (39 ft)
11.90 m – (39 ft 3 ins)
12 m   – (39 ft 6 ins)

FEI DISTANCES

Table of suggested minimum and maximum distances to be used in open combinations on level ground in normal weather conditions

Combination			
7.60 - 8.00 24'11" - 26'3"	7.50 - 7.80 24'7" - 25'7"	7.40 - 7.60 24'3" - 24'11"	7.10 - 7.40 23'3" - 24'3"
10.60 - 11.00 34'9" - 36'1"	10.50 - 10.80 34'5" - 35'5"	10.50 - 10.80 34'5" - 35'5"	10.30 - 10.40 33'9" - 34'2"
7.60 - 7.80 24'11" - 25'7"	7.30 - 7.70 24'0" - 25'3"	7.30 - 7.60 23'9" - 24'11"	7.10 - 7.40 23'3" - 24'3"
10.60 - 11.00 34'9" - 36'1"	10.40 - 10.70 34'2" - 35'1"	10.40 - 10.70 34'2" - 35'1"	10.20 - 10.40 33'6" - 34'2"
7.60 - 8.00 24'11" - 26'3"	7.40 - 7.70 24'3" - 25'3"	7.30 - 7.60 24'0" - 24'11"	7.20 - 7.40 23'6" - 24'3"
10.60 - 11.00 34'9" - 36'1"	10.40 - 10.75 34'2" - 35'3"	10.40 - 10.70 34'2" - 35'1"	10.20 - 10.50 33'6" - 34'5"
7.70 - 8.00 25'3" - 26'3"	7.60 - 7.80 24'11" - 25'7"	7.50 - 7.70 24'7" - 25'3"	
10.70 - 11.00 35'1" - 36'1"	10.50 - 10.80 34'5" - 35'5"	10.40 - 10.70 34'2" - 35'1"	

TABLE OF EASY DISTANCES IN COMBINATIONS FOR HORSES

		SECOND FENCE		
		Upright	Parallel	Staircase
FIRST FENCE	Upright	7.60 m (25 ft)	7.30 m (24 ft)	7 m (23 ft)
	Parallel	7.90 m (26 ft)	7.60 m (25 ft)	7.30 m (24 ft)
	Staircase	8.20 m (27 ft)	7.90 m (26 ft)	7.60 m (25 ft)

To convert the distance to two strides add 3.30 m (11 ft) to 3.60 m (12 ft) depending on going, etc.

TABLE OF EASY DISTANCES IN COMBINATIONS FOR PONIES

14 HANDS		SECOND FENCE		
		Upright	Parallel	Staircase
FIRST FENCE	Upright	7.30 m (24 ft)	7 m (23 ft)	6.70 m (22 ft)
	Parallel	7.60 m (25 ft)	7.30 m (24 ft)	7 m (23 ft)
	Staircase	7.90 m (26 ft)	7.60 m (25 ft)	7.30 m (24 ft)

FOR TWO STRIDES ADD 3 m (10 ft)

13 HANDS		SECOND FENCE		
		Upright	Parallel	Staircase
FIRST FENCE	Upright	6.70 m (22 ft)	6.30 m (21 ft)	6 m (20 ft)
	Parallel	7 m (23 ft)	6.70 m (22 ft)	6.30 m (21 ft)
	Staircase	7.30 m (24 ft)	7 m (23 ft)	6.70 m (22 ft)

FOR TWO STRIDES ADD 2.70 m (9 ft)

Table of easy distances in combinations for ponies, cont.

12 HANDS		SECOND FENCE		
		Upright	Parallel	Staircase
FIRST FENCE {	Upright	6 m (20 ft)	5.70 m (19 ft)	5.40 m (18 ft)
	Parallel	6.30 m (21 ft)	6 m (20 ft)	5.70 m (19 ft)
	Staircase	6.70 m (22 ft)	6.30 m (21 ft)	6 m (20 ft)
		FOR TWO STRIDES ADD 2.40 m (8 ft)		

Appendix B ◇ Notes For Holding Course Designers' Seminars

The timetable that follows was for a seminar, part of the British Horse Society's Eastern Region Training Programme in 1990, that was led by Alan Ball and the author.

This is a well-tried and successful format and makes an interesting and enjoyable day for all concerned, especially if you can organise a few horses to compete over the course at the end of the day.

BHS COURSE DESIGNERS' SEMINAR

Timetable

10.00 am	Assemble. Coffee available.
	Issue papers.
	Notes for course builders.
	Configurations of obstacles.
	Blank course. Plans of arena, to scale.
	BSJA booklet.
10.15 am	Welcome. Object of the day.
10.20 am	BSJA course designers.
	How to become a course designer.
10.35 am	Notes for course builders A B C D E.
11.00 am	*Demonstration* – 3 horses over: vertical
	parallel
	staircase
	Then: *Two Combinations*
	Staircase to vertical at 8.20 m (27 ft)
	Vertical to staircase at 7.30 m (24 ft)
11.35 am	Discussion and questions so far.
11.45 am	*Making courses.*
	The planning of a course or courses.
	Organising your arena and arena party.
	BSJA fences.
12.15 pm	Issue blank course plans.
	Form syndicates (under qualified course builders as far as possible)
12.30 pm	Syndicate leaders each plan a course with their team; then each of four courses put on blackboard.

Photo 60 *Alan Ball* (right) *and the author at the BHS Course Designers' Seminar at Herringswell in April 1990.*

> *Guideline:* 10 fences including 1 double and 1 treble
> Max. height 1.15 m (3 ft 9 ins)
> Max. spread 1.20 m (4 ft)

1.00 pm	Lunch.
1.45 pm	Alan Ball selects course to be built and supervises.
2.00 pm	Team leader of syndicate chosen builds course with 4 syndicates to act as his team.
	5th syndicate dress course with greenery and flags.
3.00 pm	Competitors walk course for Sweepstake Competition.
4.00 pm	Tea and final discussion.

NOTES FOR SHOW JUMPING COURSE DESIGNERS

A Objectives For Success

1. To produce an exciting event for spectators with a high standard of jumping and a thrilling finish.

2. To give riders a sense of achievement and satisfaction – even if they have had faults.
3. To cause a few eliminations as possible, but only get the number of clear rounds required by the type of competition.
4. To help organisers by keeping to time as much as possible.
5. To criticise your own course after the event according to how it achieved these objectives.

'Success is achieved when a course induces atmosphere and excitement among the spectators, a sense of exaltation and achievement in the riders, and confidence and enthusiasm in the horse.'

B Basic Principles

6. *Guidelines*
(a) Keep the line between fences as simple as possible.
(b) Think always of the approach to the fence.
(c) 'Vary fences between uprights, parallels and spreads.
(d) Course to work to a climax.
(e) Encourage bold jumping into a line of fences or into a combination.
(f) Be consistent size-wise through the course.
(g) Distribute fences evenly around the arena.
(h) Have a reason for every fence you set – its siting, type and size.

7. *Don'ts*
(a) Try to be too clever or original.
(b) Start novice courses away from the entrance.
(c) Put an awkward turn away from the entrance.
(d) Mix a long and a short distance in a combination.
(e) Use traps and eliminators.
(f) Break the rhythm of a course, especially in lower grades.

Note: We don't want all coursebuilders to be the same. Within these guidelines they should use their own imagination and style.

C Fence Construction

8. (a) Avoid trick fences.
   (b) Fences to give uniform resistance to a blow.
   (c) Fences to be as wide as possible (except stiles).
   (d) All poles, cups and uprights to be uniform and interchangeable.
   (e) Have plenty of fillers and 'unit fences'.
   (f) Have a colour 'motif'.
   (g) Fences in a course to be of uniform size and difficulty.
   (h) Don't make the first fence too much of a giveaway.

Note: A show jump is a notional representation of a natural fence that might be met in the country.

D Types of Fence
There are three types: Verticals/Parallels/Staircases.

9. Verticals
Gates, walls, rails, etc.

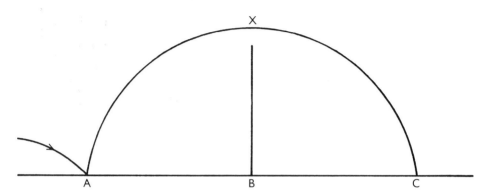

AB = BC = 1.80 m (6 ft)
D is the highest point of the horse's trajectory

10. Parallels

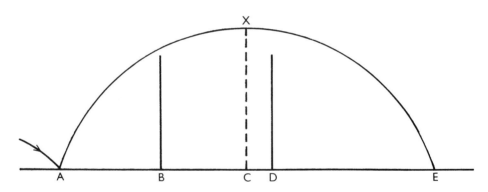

AC = CE

11. Staircases
As above, but high point moves back directly over back element.

12. Summary
Note how the highest point of the horse's trajectory gets ever further from the groundline of the obstacle. So the point of take-off must come closer to that groundline, and so the point of landing must go further out from the back element of the fence.

E Combinations

13. *General principles*
(a) Use fair, easy distances in all but advanced competitions, also at the beginning of a show.
(b) For medium classes, it is better to have big fences in combinations set at easy distances than smaller fences at awkward ones.
(c) When varying the distance be consistent. Do not in one combination have a short distance followed by a long one, or vice versa. (Except in very high class competitions.)

Note: In all our work the distance between fences is measured between the two inside elements of the fences.

14. *Upright to upright*

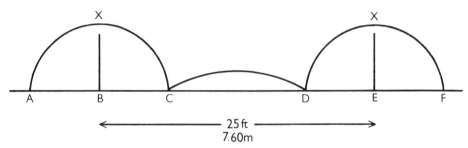

$AB = BC = DE = EF$

15. *Parallel to parallel*

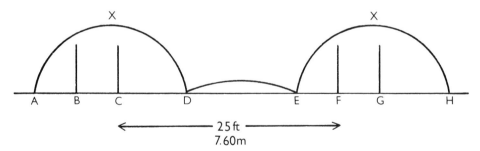

CD is greater than EF. The horse lands further out from the first fence, so its single stride brings it closer to the base of the second, which is the right place to take off at a parallel.

16. *Staircase to staircase*
CD is much greater than EF. This is an extension of what happens with two parallels. The far out landing over the first fence followed by one stride brings the horse right into the base of the second fence from where it can easily tackle this triple bar.

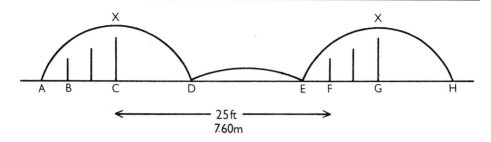

TABLE OF EASY DISTANCES IN COMBINATIONS FOR HORSES

		SECOND FENCE		
		Upright	Parallel	Staircase
FIRST FENCE	Upright	7.60 m (25 ft)	7.30 m (24 ft)	7 m (23 ft)
	Parallel	7.90 m (26 ft)	7.60 m (25 ft)	7.30 m (24 ft)
	Staircase	8.20 m (27 ft)	7.90 m (26 ft)	7.60 m (25 ft)

To convert the distance to two strides add 3.30 m (11 ft) to 3.60 m (12 ft) depending on going, etc.

For ponies – reduce per height group by: 30 cm (1 ft) for 14 hh, by 90 cm (3 ft) for 13 hh, and by 1.50 m (5 ft) for 12 hh.

F Distances Between Fences, Water Jumps

18. Distance between fences

(a) Standard distances for normal going in multiples of 3.50 m (12 ft)
   i.e.   14.50 m : 18.00 m : 21.50 m : 25.00 m : 28.50 m
         48 ft : 60 ft : 72 ft : 84 ft : 96 ft

(b) The greater the distance, the less critical it becomes.

(c) The closer the distance, the more attention should be paid to the nature of the fence – upright, parallel, spread. E.g. triple bar to vertical at 14.50 m (48 ft) will ride short.

(d) The state of the going and the type of competition will affect these distances. Heavy going will make them very long.

(e) The angle of descent affects the length of the stride after landing. The steeper the landing the shorter the next stride.

(f) Slope has a big effect on distance, which should be increased by about 30 cm (1 ft) in 6 m (20 ft) on a slight downward slope, and decreased accordingly on an upward slope. This also applies in combinations.

19. *Water jumps (BSJA Rule 139)*
(a) Must be at least wider than they are long.
(b) Water must be fairly deep.
(c) Sides of the jump should be clearly defined – shrubs and flowers.
(d) The lath clearly painted white and tilted towards the take-off.

20. *Water jumps in relation to other fences*
(a) Measuring the distance to or from a water jump is done by measuring to or from the high point of the horse's trajectory and not the lath marking the edge of the water.
(b) When placing jumps before or after the water subtract 1.5 m (5 ft) from the standard distance
    i.e. 20.40 m : 24.00 m : 27.00 m (on good going)
          67 ft : 79 ft : 91 ft

G The Course Plan

21. *General principles*
(a) Object is to obtain good jumping and a thrilling finish.
(b) Each fence to have a fair and sensible approach.
(c) Line taken by a normal competitor to produce fluent, rhythmical round.
(d) Avoid traps and eliminators.
(e) Distribute fences evenly around the arena with a big test in front of the main stand.
(f) Include at least one change of direction.
(g) The course to proceed to a climax.
(h) Fences to be kept constant in height and difficulty.
(i) Vary the fences between uprights, parallels and staircases throughout the course.

22. *Course plan should show*
(a) Location of entrance and exit.
(b) Start and finish lines.
(c) Length of course.
(d) Numbers of obstacles, their type, and the direction in which they are to be jumped.
(e) Compulsory turning points (a bad thing).
(f) The marking system used and the speed.
(g) Time allowed : time limit.
(h) Obstacles for jump-off. (Distance, speed and time allowed in jump-off.)

23. *Description of the jumps*
When the course plans are printed, it is a good idea to have a table attached to it for issue to the section leaders in the arena party, and to the commentator. The table shows:

Fence No	Description	Height	Width	Distance from previous fence
1	Brush and rail	1.20 m (4 ft)	—	—
2	Parallel bars	1.20/1.30 m (4 ft/4 ft 3 ins)	1.30 m (4 ft 3 ins)	25 m (82 ft)

H Putting up the Course

24. Material
(a) To put up a big course you need at least:

    (i)   64 good (metal) uprights
    (ii) 55 matching poles (4 m long is excellent) and 120 matching cups
    (iii) Plenty of good 'fillers' such as brush of all sizes, low walls, garden balustrades, coops, etc.
    (iv) A number of 'complete unit' fences.

(b) Uniformity of construction is essential.
(c) The wider the fences are, the better.
(d) Discard 'traps' and eliminators. All fences should require a similar blow to dislodge them. Do not fix them so tight as to be dangerous (especially gates and planks).
(e) Try and keep material as light as possible. The arena party have to carry tons of it about every day.

Note: All material should be ready *before* a visiting course designer arrives.

25. The set-up
(a) Ideal is three teams of four people each with a team leader who knows the form.
(b) With a good set up like this, it is just possible to prepare a course for a big event in two hours – three is better.
(c) When putting up your course, don't let your course plan make you too rigid. Here, experience and flair can improve a course beyond belief. Use your eyes and imagination to ensure that the course rides well. The lie of the ground may persuade you to make alterations.
(d) Course designer measures and marks with poles. Teams follow behind using their description of the jumps and build. Course designer then adjusts.

26. Fence construction
(a) The obstacles should be strong and impressive in appearance (FEI).
(b) This needs a pinch of salt and sensible interpretation.
(c) Specialities for each particular show. Show organisers look around to collect these.
(d) Cups – all standard – should never contain more than about one third of the pole. Gates should either be hung on circular rests, or, if squared rests are used, they should rest on a flat cup.

(e) Don't be too garish with colours. The use of flowers and shurbs is recommended, but dead and drooping flowers are worse than nothing. Plastic flowers are fine and silk or other material even better.

(f) Fillers should fit exactly under standard poles.

27. Flags

(a) Boundary flags at an obstacle mark the limits between which a horse must jump.

(b) Start line between 6 m (20 ft) – 25 m (82 ft) from jump.

(c) Finish line between 15 m (50 ft) and 25 m (82 ft).

28. Measuring the course

(a) 'The line normally followed by the horse'.

(b) Use this opportunity to check the construction and flagging of every fence.

I Types of Course

29. There are three types: Normal/Speed/Puissance.

30. Normal

(a) Generally Table A with one or more jumps-off.

(b) Well constructed formidable jumps – flowing line between.

(c) Should provide sufficient clear rounds to provide an exciting jump-off. How many clear rounds do you want? Why? How can you achieve this?

31. Speed

(a) NOT a mad gallop over fixed low fences!!!!!

(b) Include several changes of direction.

(c) Think of the difference between Table A4 and Table C. A4 is like a jump-off in the first round. Table C is a pure speed 'Parcours de Chasse'.

(d) Fences sufficiently big to make competitors think and ride, but not so big that crowd excitement is lost, especially in 'fun classes'.

(e) The line to be fair. The placing of the other obstacles can make a test more interesting.

(f) Course designer must understand the problems he sets.

32. Puissance

(a) Big, imposing fences, totally unrelated to each other (i.e. far apart or not on one line).

(b) Start with the siting of your final jump-off fences (which *must* be completely unrelated to one another) and work from there.

(c) The fences used for the barrages to be particularly wide, and to go to great heights without becoming hollow or becoming dangerous because of too much material.

UPRIGHT OR VERTICAL OBSTACLES & VARIANTS

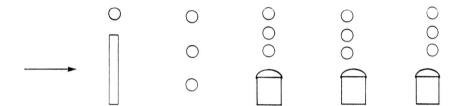

OXER OR PARALLEL OBSTACLES ASCENDING

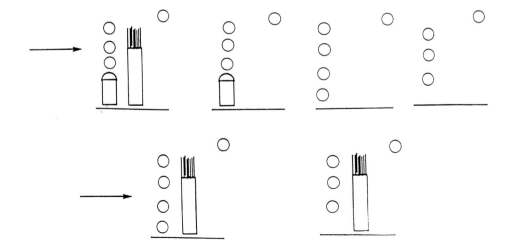

OXER OR PARALLEL OBSTACLES SQUARE

TRIPLE BAR OR STAIRCASE OBSTACLES

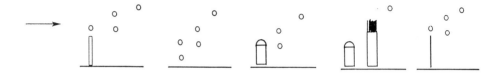

HOG'S BACK

DITCHES, EITHER DRY OR WITH WATER

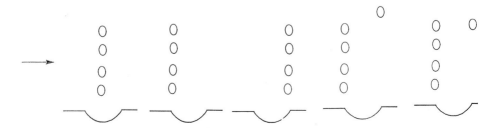

Appendix D ◇ *Exercises and Gymnastics*

The idea behind this appendix is to use some of the information given earlier to enable riders and instructors to set exercises that are beneficial to the horse.

No exercise, especially one set for a young horse, should demand too great a physical or mental effort. At all stages of schooling you should always realise that if your horse stops you have made a bad mistake.

TROTTING POLES

So, let us start at the bottom with trotting poles. Before doing any exercise it is a good idea to think what you are trying to achieve. First start with a single pole. The first time a horse crosses it he has negotiated his first jump – even if he has only walked over it. The objects of walking and trotting over a single pole are:

- To let the horse learn to adjust his own stride to negotiate an obstacle.
- To increase his range of experience.
- To encourage him to be bold.
- To stimulate activity of his hock joints.

Do not put down too many poles to start your work. Begin with two, then three, then maybe four if your horse is doing well and enjoying the work. Never go on too long – you must end on a good note. There is no hard-and-fast rule about distance between trotting poles, but they are roughly 1.20–1.50 m (4–5 ft) apart. First find the distance that best suits your horse and then teach it to complete the exercise with shorter (more collection) and longer distances. Do not *ride* the exercise, and always do rising not sitting trot so as not to put too much strain on the back. You do nothing except keep your horse straight – he must equate the stride and distance for himself.

THE FAN

Placing two poles in a fan on the ground (Photos 61–64) is a very good exercise. It is ridden on the circle. The rider must ride very accurately to come at the poles at the right place at the right angle. The horse has to think much more about where he is putting his feet as any deviation in the approach will alter the distance between the poles. The young horse is also learning to bend around the rider's inside leg. The poles

Photos 61–64 *Richard Williams and Persian Measure demonstrate the fan trotting poles. Note the increased activity of the hocks in Photo 62. Rising trot is important.*

Photo 64   *The mare is nicely flexed to the right.*

Photos 65–68 *Richard Williams and Persian Measure going down a grid. In Photo 66 the mare folds up her hind legs really well and lands exactly midway (1.80 m/6 ft) between the two fences.*

Photo 68   *Again, the mare folds up well and clearly does not want to touch a fence.*

are set at an angle of about 75° in the pictures, but you can suit yourself and vary the angle to keep rider and horse alert.

THE GRID

Next the grid. A very good exercise is a series of poles about 3.60 m (12 ft) apart. This is demonstrated by Richard Williams in Photos 65–68. The line on the ground is 1.80 m (6 ft) from each of the two fences. As with the trotting poles, you must vary the distance to teach the horse to lengthen or shorten. These poles are about 60 cm (2 ft) high. You can make them lower or higher to suit horse and rider. But a series of, say, six or more of these is a jolly good test of a young horse and well worth doing if you are trying out a horse with a view to purchase. If he can go down a line without touching a pole you are more likely to be looking at a potential jumper than if he taps them all the way down. I was pleased with the way the mare folded up her legs when jumping the exercise.

THE FUNNEL

This is discussed in Chapter 2 and demonstrated in Photos 8 and 9 on page 23. It is a very good exercise indeed for a horse that drags his hind legs over a fence.

GYMNASTICS

There are endless variations and gymnastics that can be built to help solve many different problems. Fig. D1 is a typical exercise. It consists of four poles on the ground, 3 m to a jump (say two crossed poles at 45 cm (1 ft 6 ins)), a bounce of 3.60 m (10 ft) to crossed poles at 60 cm (2 ft), then one stride of 6 m (20 ft) to a low parallel. With this basis you can ring the changes as much as you like. If your horse is not going forward sufficiently you can start with the distances as suggested here and gradually lengthen them to encourage the horse to increase impulsion. If your horse is running or jumping flat or not picking up his legs, you can shorten the distances a little, use the funnel at some or all the jumps, and ask him to stretch over quite wide (1.40–1.50 m/ 4 ft 6 ins–5 ft), low parallels.

You always need someone on the ground when using these exercises. Then you can adjust the distances and heights to solve the particular problems of your horse. Never leave the same exercise up for more than one or two days. Make constant changes so that your horse learns to think about what he is doing. In this way he will become more careful and able to help out when you are in difficulties.

| 1.50 m | 1.50 m | 1.50 m | 3 m | 3.60 m | 6 m |
| 5 ft | 5 ft | 5 ft | 10 ft | 12 ft | 20 ft |

Fig. D1

THE CIRCLE

Figure D2 shows an exercise on a 30 m (100 ft) circle. Like the fan on the ground, this is an excellent way of getting a rider to ride straight and accurately on a circle. The horse should always be at 90° to a line drawn from the centre of the circle.

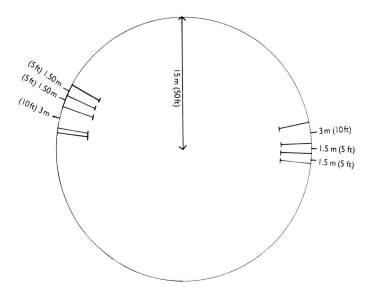

Fig. D2

RIGHT ANGLES

Figure D3 shows a very good trotting exercise. It demands a lot of control and balance and teaches a horse to pay attention to the rider. It can be jumped in either direction. It can be varied by changing the angles at which the jumps are placed as well as by the distance they are from one another.

This shape also makes a good exercise with three pairs of trotting poles placed in similar positions.

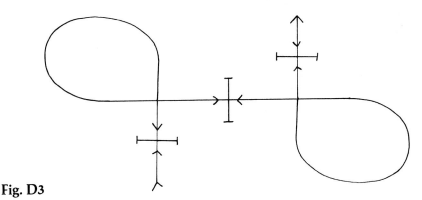

Fig. D3

ANGLE JUMPING

Figure D4 shows another good control exercise with a single first fence in a two-stride double with three alternative second fences. The difficulty of this can be increased by how you place the two outside fences. Of course the distance depends on the size of the fences, but if they are anything from 1.10 m (3 ft 6 ins) upwards, the normal two stride distances may be used.

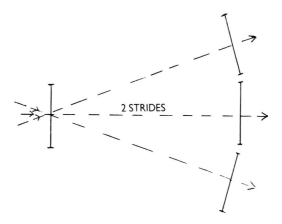

Fig. D4

POLE ON THE GROUND

Figure D5 shows a pole on the ground placed about 2.70 m (9 ft) in front of a 1.20 m (4 ft) parallel. This is not something for beginners and no one should jump it on their own. It does two things. It really makes a horse back off and fold up the legs, and it also makes a horse that is jumping flat bascule properly over the fence.

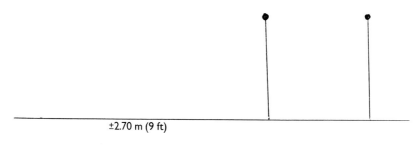

±2.70 m (9 ft)

Fig. D5

These are just some of the many exercises that a good trainer can use. They are really unlimited but if you start with these you will soon find variations to keep the interest of horse and rider going. Provided that you remember the importance of changing the layout every time you school your horse (or your pupil if you are an instructor) neither horse nor rider will ever be bored.

Index